COLORADO
MOTHER OF RIVERS

Water Poems

by

Justice Greg Hobbs

2/2006

Colorado Foundation for Water Education
Denver, Colorado

Cover photographs by Eric Wunrow (©2005, Dallas Divide, San
Juan Mountains), ericwunrow.com and Emmett Jordan (©2005,
South Platte River).

Proceeds from the sale of this book support the work of the
Colorado Foundation for Water Education.

Poems in this book have first appeared in *High Country,* the maga-
zine of the Philmont Staff Association; *High Country News; Uni-
versity of Denver Water Law Review; Environmental Law* of the
Northwestern School of Law; *The legal Studies Forum; Denver Uni-
versity Law Review; The Colorado Lawyer; Colorado River Compact
Symposium Proceedings,* Water Education Foundation; *Headwa-
ters,* Colorado Foundation for Water Education; and *In Praise of
Fair Colorado, the Practice of Poetry, History and Judging by Justice
Greg Hobbs,* Bradford Publishing Company.

Library of Congress Catologing-in-Publication Data:
Hobbs, Gregory
Poetry/Gregory Hobbs, Jr.

ISBN 0-9754075-4-6
I Colorado—Poetry
II. Greg Hobbs
III. Title
IV. Western Water Resources
V. Natural Science Poetry

Colorado Foundation for Water Education
P.O. Box 300158
Denver, CO 80203
303-377-4433
www.cfwe.org

For my wife, Bobbie
Singer of Rivers

TABLE *of* CONTENTS

Light Hurts

Setting Out

Fire and Drought

Gathering

Essay

Foreword

POETRY MATTERS

We almost didn't make it neither. There was
nothin' for us to cut but rabbit, coyote.
Grandfathers stirred their story sticks into the
coals, said of the ice that never melts up in the
Yellowstone country. We drew buffalo on the
inside of tipi walls with cold smoke the fires
made when the old men fell quiet, and let
the children gnaw the bottom thongs...

from *They Call Me Squaw Man* (p.12)

In 1992, poet Dana Gioia asked the seminal question that shocked the poetry community, "Can Poetry Matter?" Bewildered by a contemporary poetry that found its genesis in the academics of Deconstruction and the Language poets, the everyday American increasingly abandoned the "ivory tower" reading hall for the sanctuary of the library nook and its beloved populace of Frost, Whitman, and Dickinson. Or worse, they pigeon-holed it into the domain of the academic intellectual and left poetry behind all together.

What have we forgotten about poetry? Whitman called it "The Song of Myself," Dickinson, her "Letters to the World." Finally, poetry is one man or woman's dialogue with the world. It is the recording of the brief moments of his or her life, in celebration, in mourning, in exaltation. The poet, William Stafford, describes the act of writing as "the successive discovery of cumulated epiphanies in the self's encounter with the world."[1] And sometimes, if we're lucky, the poet invites us in. And sometimes, if we're even luckier, that poet is a good man with much to teach us about humility, awe, and civility. *Colorado: Mother of Rivers* is Justice Greg Hobbs' invitation to us. Justice of the Colorado Supreme Court, water lawyer, scholar, humanitarian, loving husband, father, grandfather, and friend, Justice Hobbs takes us on a tour of a benevolent world rife with the history, culture, and soul. He is the consummate traveler—"Some days I look/out the window/ and get nothing done/but the looking" (*Out the Window,* p.43)—wide-eyed and unboundedly generous.

If Walt Whitman is the poet of America, then Justice Hobbs is a poet of Colorado—put that in capitol letters. He teaches us that poetry does matter to the poet and to the reader, whether it is a poetry of the academic institution, of the street, or of a place and its spirit. His poems are poems of place—Vallecito Creek (*Reconnoiter,* p.29), Mesa Verde (*Mesa Verde,* p.40), Firehole (*The Firehole River,* p.107), and Tin Cup (*Back Home Within a Week,* p.17). They are poems of people—Sacagawea (*I See Sacagawea,* p.8), Meriwether Lewis (*The Song of Meriwether Lewis,* p.9), the Puebloans (*Pueblo People of Mesa Verde,* p.6), Squaw Man (*They Call Me Squaw Man,* p.12), Cloyd and Will (*From the Gap,* p.28). They are poems of nature—elk-bugle (*Coming Into Fall,* p.37), stratocirrus (*Mad With The Moon,* p.83), golden banner wing (*White Moths, Yellow Butterflies,* p.84), heron (*Dance The Heron Reel,* p.22), red fox (*A Fox in Elder Berry Rain,* p.40) and caddis fly (*I Like The Feel Of A Book,* p.61). To read Justice Hobbs' poetry is to sit at the divine table of Colorado and partake of its sweetest nectars.

Colorado Mother of Rivers celebrates the land and water of Colorado and the rich human and spiritual history that continues to grow from them. As William Stafford said, "For the person who follows with trust and forgiveness what occurs to him, the world remains always ready and deep, an inexhaustible environment."[2] Justice Hobbs dips into this world again and again without pretence and reminds us of what is surely ours too:

> *Your earth is waking,*
> *I can feel your soil give*
> *to the plant of your heel,*
> *my nostrils swell with the*
> *fragrant smell of your green.*

A downslope wind pushes in
from mountain dwellings,
the prairie stirs to welcome
you. And so you go as you
came, dear friend, a blessing!

—from *Dear Friend* (p.42)

Kathryn Winograd, Ph.D
Writer's Studio
Arapahoe Community College

---

[1] Stafford, William. "Writing: The Discovery of Daily Experience." Writing the Australian Crawl 51 (Ann Arbor: The University of Michigan Press, 1978).
[2] Stafford, 20.

Introduction

OF WATERSHEDS AND WATER FOLK

You will not remember this—
the river, its blue stalks of heron,

or how I was everything to you once
at the river's edge, our walking here

on egg smooth stones like the carried heart
of the mountain, unpieced.

from *Air into Breath*[1] by Kathryn Winograd

This book you hold is over wintering. It emerges, as Colorado light grows brighter into Spring, with Kathy Winograd's graceful and intelligent foreword. What Kathy didn't say was that her book *Air Into Breath* won the 2003 Colorado Book Award for Poetry. Nor did she mention her online course for K-12 Colorado teachers, *Teaching the Poetry of Rivers.* Composed of five lesson plans, this masterpiece of the teacher's art glistens with poetry, history, culture, science, Colorado's incredible watersheds, and the people, other creatures, and landforms that inhabit them.

Since 1991, my wife Bobbie and I have taken many of Kathy's poetry courses and workshops. What a joy! Sure and inspiring, she looses the tongues and writing fingers of her students. She's passionate about the ability of each person to hear the music in the language and to write simply, concretely, figuratively and well. Once in awhile, we'll succeed in asking her to read one of her own poems. Like a river she bubbles, moans, purrs, slakes her pace, pours forth her rich economy of sensuously-intelligent metaphor. The creed she inspires: poetry is creative personal communication shaped to be read aloud in community.

I try to practice this creed. I receive many invitations to talk with citizen groups about Colorado and Western water history and culture. Often I will read a poem by Walt Whitman, Emily Dickinson, William

Stafford, or Thomas Hornsby Ferril, or one of my own. My own poem may be freshly minted from traveling through another piece of incredible landscape to get to the place of the talk, or from hearing the speakers before me, or from having breakfast, lunch, or dinner with fellow citizens before my talk. I am also called to deliver invocations, weddings, and eulogies. And I am called to explain how the law is a reflection of the customs and values of the people, as poems are.

I try to practice plain-listening and melodic-speaking. One cannot love the West, as we all do, without loving open space, truth-saying, story telling, being worthy of the place we find ourselves, building habitable dwelling places, and conserving water for all we're worth.

I refresh the taste for doing this by reading Terry Tempest Williams' *The Open Space of Democracy:* "Democracy depends on engagement, a firsthand accounting of what one sees, what one feels, and what one thinks, followed by the artful practice of expressing the truth of our times through our own talents, gifts, and vocations."[2] She's a marvelous prose-poet. In describing the great and threatened beauty of Alaska's Arctic Wildlife Refuge, her "Arctic Angel" is a tern.

> *My eyes catch the illumined wings of the tern, an Arctic tern, fluttering, foraging above the river—the embodiment of grace, suspended. The tern animates the vast indifference with its own vibrant intelligence. Black cap; blood-red beak pointed down; white body with black-tipped wings. With my eyes laid bare, I witness a bright thought in big country. While everyone is sleeping, the presence of this tern hovering above the river, alive, alert, engaged, becomes a vision of what is possible.*[3]

Another prose-poet of the West is John Wesley Powell. I include in this volume an after-dinner talk George Sibley asked me to prepare for the 2004 Gunnison Water Workshop. I ended that evening by reciting *A Colorado River Journey* (p.30). What a privilege to read Williams and Powell, to enjoy the open spaces of democracy that so animate them, to recite in my own personal and public way the vow of how each of us may find our way home—here.

I've had many a fisher-backpacker trip into such places. Brother Will, the young adult author, is a fellow Coloradan. He and his wife Jean have led many a family trip into the Weminuche Wilderness of the San Juan mountains along the great bend of the Continental Divide. Those experiences sharpen my eye for pristine detail, my ear for the sound of running water, my heart for the recording and the rendering.

Of course, some of our most accurate recorders of the Western experience are trees. I am reminded of this by a recent visit with the tree-ring researchers, and by many-a-day of being at our summer cabin in the ponderosa zone.

RING BEARERS OF THE ROCKY MOUNTAIN WEST

O, Ring bearers of the Rocky Mountain West—
Pinyon, Ponderosa, Doug Fir, Bristlecone—
packed-to-the-core tenacious recorders

You stand watch on mountain up-slopes,
foothill arroyo down-slopes,

May we borrow your driest,
your brim-full, memories?

We have need of your common signals:
for seasons of want, stay together close;
expand to greet all sufficient opportunity
in tall-grass lupine summers.

No ignorance stored in you,
the nearer we penetrate
ours relents

Community solitude. Gregarious, you spread
your knowledge concentrically, like planets
round a center fire do, unevenly. Make

a stand grandly in the place you've chosen,
populate bills of light given you.

How they shrink or swell,
you ensemble streams and rivers
marked within.

May we call your-names?
Seldom-Wanderers,
Stress-Abiders,
Constant-Conservators,
Great Divide Sentinels.

(for Connie Woodhouse, Brad Udall, Jeff Lukas, Robin Webb)

I have grouped the poems in this book with a touch thematic, though each   stands independently, I hope. Of leading significance are the historical and personal locations of a Coloradan, of one becoming a Coloradan in community amidst a challenging and beautiful landscape (*In Scarcity is the Opportunity for Community* and *Settling In*). Amidst our yearning to be in the pristine solitude of the prairie, streams, and mountains, we see the brevity of our personal existence in light of those who have passed before (*The Edge of Things*). Finding that we spend a majority of our time and place in a rapidly growing urban environment, if we look, surprisingly we find other creatures and great moments of beauty and insight (*Urban Wild Perches*). Spiritual movement and growth occurs in moving back and forth between our urban and wild perches, as the seasons turn and light becomes so bright it hurts the eyes, and dark places of our state's and our personal history also illuminate the way (*Light Hurts*). We equip ourselves only with what we need, metaphorical tents, stoves, backpacks, and set out again with determination into the Western landscape (*Setting Out*). A harsh environment intrudes as we experience personally the recurrence of fire and drought, constant features of living here (*Fire and Drought*). We find personal strength and strength in community as we listen to our teachers, the land, other creatures, and each other (*Gathering*). We get ready to pass on full of joy, wistfulness, and nostalgia for all we have been privileged to see (*Cinch My Filament*).

I dedicate these water poems to the people of Colorado and the West and, most especially, my dear wife Bobbie, my fellow walker. We thank the Colorado Foundation for Water Education for its work in water education and water literature, and for accepting our contribution to it.

I especially thank Karla Brown, executive director of the Colorado Foundation for Water Education, for the many ways she has helped to give voice to the voices of Colorado water; and Emmett Jordan for his friendship, for his co-authorship of two of the poems, and for the design and layout of this book. Emmett is an artist with camera, computer, and words. The front cover is courtesy of Eric Wunrow; thank you so much for the glory of your photography, which often appears in Water Foundation publications.

I acknowledge permission of The Smithsonian Institution Press for allowing me to quote from Joni Louise Kinsey's book, *Thomas Moran and the Surveying of the American West,* and The Island Press for permission to quote from William deBuys's collection of Powell writings, *Seeing Things Whole, The Essential John Wesley Powell.* And I thank Terry Tempest Williams and The Orion Society for permission to quote from *The Open Space of Democracy,* and Kathryn Winograd and the Ashland University Press for the quote from *Air into Breath.*

Some of the poems in this book, and many companion talks, essays, and articles about water and the West, appear in my book *In Praise of Fair Colorado, The Practice of Poetry, History, and Judging,* published by Bradford Publishing Company.

May watersheds and water folk continue to loosen our tongues and strengthen our hearts for passages yet-to-be!

Greg Hobbs
March, 2005

---

[1] Kathryn Winograd, from "River Swim," *Air into Breath* (The Ashland Poetry Press 2002) .

[2] Terry Tempest Williams, *The Open Space of Democracy* 85 (The Orion Society 2004).

[3] Id. 45.

Preface

IN THE RHYTHM OF THE RIVERS

When Powell, Hayden, Wheeler and King, embarked on their great Western surveys in the 19th Century they brought along sketchers, photographers, and painters—Holmes, Jackson, and Moran, among them. They mapped the waters and the stunning clarity that lack of water imparts to this landscape. They fired the imagination of will-be-westerners. We are still settling in.

Born to an Air Force family, I had the great fortune of living all over the West, including Alaska, California, and Texas. I grew up along the shores and rivers wherever a fisherman father and a mother who believed in blessings cared to take their four sons and daughter.

Blessings are of water and the spirit. History was my college major at Notre Dame. I've been writing poetry longer than I've been a lawyer and judge. Walt Whitman, W.B. Yeats, Emily Dickinson, Robert Frost, Thomas Hornsby Ferril, and William Stafford are poets I greatly admire. Colorado poet Kathryn Winograd is my teacher.

My wife, Bobbie, appeared to me at Philmont, the National Boy Scout Camp in northern New Mexico's Sangre de Cristo Range. We were both on summer staff there in the Sixties. Her home was Colorado. We served in the Peace Corps together. I constantly learn from her. She is the inspiration of inspirations who keeps me going.

My first law job after graduation in 1971 from Boalt Hall at the University of California, Berkeley, was clerk to U.S. Circuit Judge William E. Doyle. He served on the Colorado Supreme Court before joining the federal judiciary. I pass his picture every day in the hall outside the door of my chambers.

When I left Colorado after the clerkship to practice in San Francisco, Judge Doyle's parting reproach/challenge to me was, "Why don't you make your stand here?" I'm still standing on the strength of that question.

I came to Colorado for good in 1973, the same year my brother Will, the young-adult writer of Western adventure stories, also settled here. My professional career in water and environmental law began at the U.S. Environmental Protection Agency's new regional office. Then, at the Colorado Attorney General's Office and in private practice, I concentrated on air, water, water quality, land use, and transportation law. Governor Romer appointed me a Justice of the Colorado Supreme Court in 1996. The citizens of Colorado retained me for a ten year term starting in 1999.

I love the way that water works and sings in this land of the Great Divide. In this, as with all Coloradans, I am led by our predecessors, the Pueblo people of Mesa Verde and the Hispano settlers of the San Luis Valley. In the *Citizen's Guide to Colorado Water Law,* published in 2003 by the Colorado Foundation for Water Education, I have helped to tell how they—before the Anglo settlers—pioneered the use of water in the dry country.

We have the privilege and the responsibility of living at the headwaters of two great oceans. How we settle into this land, observing its seasons with great joy and respect, will mark our sojourn here. When we measure ourselves in relation to prairie, mesa, canyon, peaks, we begin to see how magnificently temporary we are. How we treat each other, how we express our love for the opportunity given us to live amidst these wondrous surroundings—these are the wellspring sources of our daily strength.

To the making of this book I owe great thanks to Emmett Jordan, designer of all the fine publications of the Colorado Foundation for Water Education. In contributing his work to the design of this book, he joins me in celebrating the Foundation's role in bringing the creative joy of water back home to Coloradans. I also thank Eric Wunrow for contributing his spectacular photograph of the Dallas Divide.

Working with water and playing in and along it makes you want to sing. The poems in this volume span four decades of living and working along the Great Divide. I hope you will see and hear in them many vistas and moments common to Coloradans and westerners. In the rhythm of the rivers, the West finds its most treasured experience.

COLORADO
MOTHER OF RIVERS

When I was young the waters sang
of being here before I am,
of falling sweet and soft and slow
to berry bog and high meadow.
And held me in her lap and cooed
the willow roots, the gaining pools,
and called me through bright dappled grass
and called me O, My Shining One;

And shaped a bed to lay me on
and played the flute so high and clear.
And shape the stones to carry me,
when I am young and full of fight
for roaring here and roaring there,
for pouring torrents in the air.
When I am young as mountain snow
in crag and cleft and cracked window;

I call the green-backed cutthroat trout,
I call the nymph and hellgrammite,
I call the hatch to catch a wind,
I call upon the mountain track;
I call the scarlet to the jaw
as morning calls her own hatchlings,
call Yampa, White, the Rio Grande,
San Juan, the Platte, the Arkansas.

*(in celebration of the 30th year
of Colorado's instream flow law)*

In Scarcity
the Opportunity for Community

PUEBLO PEOPLE OF MESA VERDE

You want to know where water's precious,
where every scoop of dirt's a prayer of life;
and tomorrow's blessing—carried in a pot

Of clay is a source of wonder up a slope
a thousand years away—perch upon
a buried kiva's rim and take within the

Arcing southeast sun this light they saw—
you see—and may you keep this light
within and speak it openly;

They worked and loved, like we, this
land, this calling, this Mesa Verde.

WEDDING AT HOVENWEEP

Two canyons, two towers,
one of the sun,
one of the moon,
from distant geographies
these two canyons
converge

Where—now—
these two towers
stand—
Together—
at the head of the floor
of each

These canyons hold
the gouging and the leveling
of their tributaries
that, shaping them,
have made their features
singular

Between the walls
of their different understandings,
in the niches and the crevices,
voices feed and murmur
children/turkeys/families/dogs
while these two towers stand

A flute shall play,
and through the earthen
windows of these
two figures stretching
light of evening,
light of midday.

ADMIRES DUCKS

Who would walk
and float and fly,
who dwells within
each element,
water, earth and air,

Admires ducks.
How the Ancient Ones
could splice a human torso
to a wing'ed brain
and light a fire.

I SEE SACAGAWEA

I see Sacagawea on the silver dollar.
She carries an infant in a blanket sling
around her shoulders,
her hair sweeps back beyond
the infant from a high forehead
and confident visage.

An eagle soars on the other side
among the stars. Her touch has turned
the silver dollar bronze
as bite of shining mountains
turns bronze the prairie grass
and cottonwood.

She travels West with Virginians
and a Frenchman, what shall
they see when we arrive
to greet them in that country
vast between a mighty wingspan
and her lovely face?

THE SONG OF MERIWETHER LEWIS

Out there
another mountain range
out beyond the stars.

Out there beyond the stars
another prairie tall
out there

Out beyond the stars
another river falls.
Out there

Out beyond the stars
I'll be going there.
Out there

Out beyond the stars.

LEWIS AND IVES

A River always bends its course against
the confident.

Said the President, "Your mission is single,
the direct water communication from sea to sea
formed by the Missouri."

Lewis holding forth on foot
crossed the Bitter Roots.

And Lieutenant Ives,
who from tide to source would power
up the Colorado,

Foundered on a rock,
his steamer split apart.
"Ours has been the first, and will
doubtless be the last to visit
this profitless locality."

Just up the pike
Las Vegas lights.

ACEQUIA MADRE

She is bubbling
when first she runs down
the arroyo sandals flopping
onto the sagebrush plain
waving and exclaiming about

The distant Rio Grande
and La Sierra gleaming back
hair, soles, toes, teeth
harking time she digs in
finger-molded mounds

Bright green tendrils grow
breasts and belly swelling
full like melting snow
her voice sounds

High and pure.

ACEQUIA MADRE IS SHUT

At field's corner
old man cottonwood bends
over the top strand

Dragging gnarly elbows along the ditch.

Jack rabbit bellies under
from twisted claw doe hair hangs
skiff of snow raptly holds inert rows

And the iced-up wheel of a headgate waits.

Across the plot like an open wound
jagged laterals
cut

Acequia Madre is shut.

THEY CALL ME SQUAW MAN

They call me squaw man. On account
of the Cheyenne woman I live with.
There weren't no other women here
when I came out. Her people took me
in. We'd skinned along the cottonwood
bottoms, at Big Timbers on the Arkansas,
set our poles and wrapped our hide tight
to the raw smoke opening at the top,
strangle berries was already freezin'.

That's when the Pathfinder come through,
says he discovered South Pass, crossed
the Sierra in a big snow, liberated Californi'.
Says he knows where the Railroad's got to go,
from St. Louis out the Arkansas, up and over
the 38th Parallel.

I says to him, Don't go up there. We been
chunkin' ice out of river edges since
September just to get a drink. Up in the hills
deer and bear been growin' more than usual
hair, and it ain't strange ten feet or more
of snow up there with early signs like this.

"Old Fool," he says. "I've done it all before.
Follow me, Men, don't listen. Just up
and over the other side to California!"

He tries the San Juans in December,
gets hisself and the men stuck in a notch
between the Rio Grande and whatever.
Bogs down at Christmas. The mules was
freezin' in their tracks and there wasn't
any eatin' left a civilized man can mention
once they was down and the flesh stripped.
The Pathfinder skedaddles out of there
to Taos and Californi'.

There's ten men didn't. Left their marks
on the bark where a Griz can't reach
and claw when the snow melts.

We almost didn't make it neither. There was
nothin' for us to cut but rabbit, coyote.
Grandfathers stirred their story sticks into the
coals, said of the ice that never melts up in the
Yellowstone country. We drew buffalo on the
inside of tipi walls with cold smoke the fires
made when the old men fell quiet, and let
the children gnaw the bottom thongs. River
finally loosed and we scraped into the Sand Hills.

My woman died of the pox. Chivington gutted
her family a year later. The railroad's chasin'
the old Smoky Hill trail into Denver. They've
carved through Cheyenne for the trans-continental.
I spend my days hackin' around Fort Lyon,
the white people tell their children

Don't go near that squaw man!

CODE OF THE PASSING THROUGH PEOPLE

Pack our wagons, so the axles ride a little
higher than the wagon-tearing stones, not so high
a capsize-wind will blow over the edge all we
carefully stowed, or in mire-hole sink beyond

Resurrection. Pack only what we're needing and
hope chest bear for when we homestead arrive, and there's
cause for remembering what of our ancestors
at table before us spread, to remember theirs.

And do not expect what we do not earn, and thank
always for what is given us. And do not waste
what tomorrow we may need, or blind to another's
need, in grace and privilege, we may choose to freely

Give. Sharpen our axes, oil our guns, for they are
tools, like the hammer, nail, stool, hand, and milking pail,
lamp, wick, candle, planed-off plank and any good book,
needle, thread, spindle, spool, crank, flume and headgate wheel,

Self-defense a right, but never to pick a fight
or intimidate or disregard innocents
or refuse to forgive or ask for forgiveness.
Insist that conscience begins in living it, string

String, every string, so every string plays of future
well-being. How the red wing blackbird morning sings
and barn owl hunts the fluttering evening, cherish
every creature for that creature's form of speaking

And every intonation and form of being.
And when we borrow another person's strength or
natural feature, honor and repay, in how we
transforming live and love and better pass on through.

POWELL'S RUN

Spread beyond the eye and senses,
Powers and Principalities,
every feature finely etched
tower, ridge, toehold
granary scat stashed,
disemboweled mist,
scrabble crust
red porridge downpour,
cathedrals, thrones,
caverns, furnaces,
hanging gardens,
cretaceous creatures
massed in dancing curtain
rims of the solid slipping sea,
turquoise tributaries so pure
paradise seems a reflection,
schist chasm of the plunging
night, lurch of vertigo in merciless
cold and heat unbearable,
roaring so complete no power
or principality can compete,
round a bend run down, down,
down from Lee Ferry to Havasu
Surge home again.

MAPPERS

St. Louis blinking out
mule currents to a sea of grass
through the Mandan land
launched upon the plains,
like ships beyond the Hesperides

Adrift the willow brakes
and Boomer-Baked
sweet for ruby-throated wind
Arikaree.
Like stinging nettles, bees,

Mappers of wild fantasy
into Nebraska, the Dakotas, Kansas, blunder.
And how might Oregon pretend to send for
Powell, Hayden, Wheeler, King,
so many fathers lost
between the Platte and Williamette?

Children peek them out,
children of their children,
creeks that trickle
through the streets
Romero, Carlin,
Petros, Hay, Berardi, Rhodes

BACK HOME WITHIN A WEEK

He came by way of Tincup
from the diggin's up in Creede,
the days of slammin' iron,
the nights of knowin' greed,
he's been through every camp
Telluride to Ten Mile Creek,
there's one sure place he's goin',
back home within a week.

He's got to keep on leavin',
there's nothin' can suffice,
the hole that's deeper dug
has findin' as its price,
if not in Tabor's meadow
then on Stratton's Cripple Creek,
there's one sure place he's goin',
back home within a week.

The Rockies have a cure
for those who brave the West,
a man get's kind of crazy
all that coughin' in his chest,
the River keeps on fallin',
his luck has run a leak,
there's one sure place he's goin',
back home within a week.

Now the moon is made of metal
and the sun's a glowin' heap,
the groanin' of a man
wakes nothin' from his sleep,
not bones beneath the ground
nor snows upon the peak,
there's one sure place he's goin',
back home within a week.

COME IN, THEN!

Come in, then!
A Colorado snow falls
on your topcoat, you may
shake it off over this threshold.
Enter, please. Dinner awaits
after. You may want to rest
in this anteroom by the fire, you
have traveled hard to get here.
Over the Palmer Divide wasn't it?
from the Pike's Peak country,
by way of the Smoky Hill route
previously? Turn round. Make
a small hole in the cold of the glass
and look through. Snow is letting up.
Your children will be putting theirs
to bed soon and telling stories
they invented from yours.

LUDLOW STATION

At the end of the plains they came,
the immigrants,
to the long low hills of Ludlow
along the Purgatoire,
"Spics" and "Wops" and "Micks,"
from the tents below they could
not see the Spanish Peaks.

Beneath the silver snows they tore
the stone for chunks of coal
had no home that was their own
but lived in tents with coat of black
to warm their lungs as wages
from the CF&I.

Strikes that founded Denver Town
along the Platte and Cherry Creek
grew fortunes for the few who knew
but would not recognize these battered
few who struck to feed their families.

So the Guard did ride to Trinidad
with threats and epithets about their
foreign birth, still they would not bear
beneath the ground or let the coking fires
burn for Rockefeller or for Welborn.

A train runs down from Denver Town
with Pinkertons on an Easter Holiday,
Spring has swept the tracks of snow,
when engines slow at Ludlow
families run from Gatling guns,
burn and die for the CF&I.

At the end of the plains they came,
the immigrants,
to the long low hills of Ludlow
along the Purgatoire,
from the tents below they rose
unto the Spanish Peaks.

SETTLING IN

FLOOD OF THE BIG THOMPSON,
A REPORT

Big Thompson flooded over last night.
Visitors said they didn't realize rain
could do a thing so vast. Residents
called it worst in memory. Spokesperson
for the Water Conservancy District estimated
damage to the Project in Millions. Guard
set up a command post below the Narrows
for counting of the Dead and Wounded.
All day ABC dissected Leads. Governor
observed the Centennial. Mountains
watched impassively.....(more to follow).

DANCE THE HERON REEL

Coming to the water trail
from the rush of April-May
to the hush of December day
has such a chance.

Those sleight degrees that warm
the chill of covers off
or stump a cultured vine,
will the water boarders cross?

In the limits of a rill
sleeps a mountain with the sky
and all who hope for banks to fill.
Why a shovel was invented
to turn this soil so
is to spot a bend of river
once pretended for a field.

Ever may a being feel, nostrils to the wind,
To hold against a rainbow plough
And dance the heron reel!

STEGNER

On wheels born Western man
he warned of that mobility
from which he sprang,
unbridled optimism and the roar
of V-8 horses loosed upon the arid
vast and open space,
free land and freer water

Of the Reclamation Bureau he swore
as a blooming desert Mormon might
swear to God of locusts,
cranky cast iron stove he smoked
more we stoked his heat

Matter of lenses, I think,
his were not fit for preaching—
more for teaching in
a living room.

Themes that marked him most

One-armed Major's headlong
river plunge, careless harvest
of the wilderness, natural law
of limits, the good of settling in

Died in Santa Fe
not by hanging rope or pistol shot—
myths he fought cantankerous about—
but by Ford or GM truck
like many a Western man struck down

He in the line of duty,
a peace officer,
posting speed control signs
on the borders of our frontier minds:

Wanted
A True Civilization
Not A Ruthless Occupation
Disguised As Romantic Myth

SECOND CREEK

From every limb and flower
this lovely morning drips
power. Limber pine and petal
I shall gain the ridge,
hear the wind begin
to blow.
Lung by lung,
tarn by tarn, lichen
blackened rock shall lead us on.

Above the double yellow
ribbon road, First and Second Creeks,
I wonder on the age of cornices,
how they build to greet
the really heavy ice?

Most amaze, that never summer
see, yet hold their ground,
tuft of grasses,
fervently.

Cache that packers stashed,
might it be as searing pain
or quietly, to be lifted
by a cloud, held, then
dropped

As curtain cumuli?
Against a cairn
precarious I
lean.

I'VE SEEN THE MOUNTAINS FALLING

I've seen the mountains falling,
heard the mighty canyons ring
with Colorado thunder
and clear blue mountain streams,
I've seen the nights grow brighter
and the days just shine in gold,
been looking for El Dorado
in the mountain of my dreams.

I hear the eagles calling,
see torches in the sky,
went off to Colorado,
had a gleaming in my eye,
there I found my measure
was a bird upon the wing
and the mountains' greatest treasure
is the way the aspen sing.

I guess you might get crazy
thinking you're going to die,
you drive your body pounding,
waste beauty on your way,
you turn your only fortune
into gambling your life away,
when El Dorado's being
on a Colorado Day.

I wish I'd seen the world,
been a woman and a man,
felt the grip of dry starvation
and sailed the Rio Grande,
I'd be a farmer, mountaineer,
write a book about the mind,
but lay me down a fossil
in Colorado land.

DIVIDE

The mystery of a divide
is this, you can stand on opposites
and not lose your balance.

Draw a straight line from the sky
through the middle of your forehead,
half of you belongs to the other ocean.

Half your mind and half your heart,
you share downstream equally
and never drift apart.

RED ROCKS

We gathered here for farming,
for mining and for trees,
came to work the traplines
and gold upon our knees,
we prayed to God for guidance
and mapped a thousand peaks,
built the gleaming cities
and plugged the wildest creeks.

The Rockies have a hold of us
and of our ancestry,
plains and rivers tell us
there's granite in the sea,
an ocean where the canyons are,
each rock a history,
Colorado is as old as us
as young as we might be.

Now each of us has had a day
we've done our best and worst,
said our share of lying
and placing mankind first,

we've but to see that lupine
is the future at our feet
and marmots running sprightly
over Rocky Mountain peaks.

Thunder's booming sharply
across the plains below,
we see the lightning flashing,
hear the wind begin to blow,
mountains all are burning
in sunset's awesome glow,
it's all up there before us
in clouds piled up like snow.

GRANDFATHER

Grandfather, I think I know why
you keep repeating the stories,
saying them is another trip out
of Kansas to Pike's Peak or the
Grand Canyon, swaying across
the land rising into the clouds
with eggs and pancakes, your
Mother talking you along before
you ever set out. And now you're
one hundred and ten years old,
imagine that! And when the current's
talking with your tongue just beneath
the surface, when I close my eyes
and grasp my knees as close to you
as banks permit, I hear you sound
every word its bubble of oxygen.

OLD BENT'S FORT

I ride with my son along the Arkansas
from Avondale through Boone, La Junta,
Las Animas and Lamar, we talk of William
Bent and Charlie Autobees, how they
settled with the River, one on the north
bank in American Territory, the other
just across, where Mexico started
or ended, depending on how you see
the idea of countries starting and ending.
Each of them turned the river onto the
land, so to eat while the sky hung out
over the prairie. Dan and I pass to
the ramparts, reconstructed. Bent
and his Cheyenne bride lend us their
eyes for looking through the cottonwoods
to the River, smoke curls up from the plaza.

FROM THE GAP

"We can hump it in
on a long weekend,"
Will called to say.

I'd just finished *Beardance*
and how Cloyd fed the cubs
with fish he'd caught from Lost.

Going back to the sky
with your brother
and a Kelty pack
feels like a native
tugging on the line.
"Sure," said I gratefully.

At Vallecito we loaded up
on black Panthers, two-a-piece,
and bungee-strapped a cooking grate.

Renewing rites of a man,
our father.
"Horsed 'em!"
he explained when
one of us would lose a big one.
So we bust in
on sore feet trying.

Disassembled a rod is useless,
but grooved and fitted snug
it's that part of an arm
that connects a man
with higher beings.

From the gap above Irving
Will and I climbing
spotted where Cloyd
fished for bears.

RECONNOITER

We pause at the junction, Will and me.

Behind us down-canyon ten miles Vallecito Creek empties into flat
water. Where Piece-of-Texas cabins nestle cheek to jowl, wooden
butterflies stick to the door of each garage.

We aim to bushwhack.

Will believes there must be a gap between Irving Peak and Mt. Oso. I
don't know. We've crinkled up the U.S.G.S. topographical map trying to
imagine whether a passage or a precipice awaits.

So we saddle up our Kelty packs twenty-eight years out from the Muir
Trail break-in trip. Just how the Divide might let us through its guardian
phalanx can only be tried.

A COLORADO RIVER JOURNEY

Ready for Lee's Ferry, we pile in the van
hoping wrong the brochures, for how can
they say all it can weigh, 30 pound luggage?
The boats of the day are lined to the shore,
there's one that's a Hatch, how lucky we are,

We watch with amazement our crew of just
two. Chris moves about with the feet of a cat,
he's here, he's there, and that will be that. We
load and we board, John's the boatman in charge.
He first gives us all a most serious stare, then he

Forswears, "It may not look like it, but we're
out of here!" We're up and away, out on the
River, we hear about Lee and his problems
with the law, he was the only one done in
for the Mountain Meadow Massacre,

Funny, it seems, just one man could cause such
a misdeed, nevertheless, 'twas he who paid,
paid with his head. The Roaring Twenties
give such a thrill, water in teeth over our
ears, but we get not a spill. The rapids

Are fun and supper is great, where else
could you find a more glorious steak?
We learn the rules are few and wise, help
where you can, watch out for each other,
pee in the stream and climb for the can,

It seems the Park Service thinks a human
should take whatever it takes to leave
a camp clean. In the morning it's eggs,
how you want them to be, and plenty
of ripe cowboy coffee. We hike to

Some ruins of the gone ancient ones,
they came here in summer, the same so
for we. We see their water garden, Vesey's
Paradise, the Little Colorado is also a jewel,
a mix of turquoise and mother of pearl.

We put on life vests like they were diapers for
dopes and slide on our rumps through the
pools and the bumps. Splash-grins to
our faces and bruises on tushes, guess
being free is "Butts to the Board," our

Boatman's command with big rapids at
hand. This Captain we know has a thing
about Hance, it holds him in thrall to the
shape of a grimace. If demon there be
deep under the current, it's his to surmount

By running above it. They get us on through,
our hell of a crew, we cheer and we cheer
the demon's surprise at the skill of our men
and their hold on the tiller. We hope in our
age to company with grace.

To name one-by-one or in bunches of two
all the rapids we've run is to read you the
journal of John Wesley Powell. Their
names have the names of the most
precious of stones, the names of some

People who the River calls home….>>>>
Line up for the tongue, watch out for the
sleepers, latch your hands to the bundle,
and now there's a dip—and now it's a tumble—
waves all ajumble you flow past the holes,

Thank God for the roar and profound solitude!
I'd sing you a song of desert's hot breath,
of songs in the stream go bubbling along,

of herons on beaches, sheep upon ledges,
I'd sing you the raven on the stony tall butte,

The spiny shine lizard near under your foot,
I'd sing you the nights when the stars are all
out, and your bed is the sand and you're glad
you're alive. You don't care you can't sleep
because the morning is coming, and her

Beauty's so deep. She welcomes the dark
with open eyelashes and the stars disappear,
and always the song of the River you'll carry
deep in your heart and away far from here.

Walks that are many, so high in the air, on
Rock that is weathered a billion-half years,
the Falls are so mighty and sing of reprieve,
how sweet it can be to sing liberty, how this
Country has grown to leave this preserved,
this strength and this glory, this land's mystery.

You may call it Shinumo, you may call it Havasu,
Matkatamiba, Elves Chasm, but what's in a name
when the name it shall be is called Paradise?
I know I've been stinky, I know I've been sad,
the joy of new friends is a joy that I've had

Running the River on Hatch Number 3
with a hell of a crew and the greatest of food,
safe in my vest, with some sleeping to do, bid
us all to each other the fondest adieu. One
final word: keep your Butts to the Board,

You can hardly believe it, but you're not
out of here, no matter you go, for the
River is home once you've been here
and the running is good and the
running is good.

COLORADANS

To each of us
the land, the air, the water,
mountain, canyon, mesa, plain,
lightning bolts, clear days with no rain,

At the source of all thirst,
at the source of all thirst-quenching hope,
at the root and core of time and no-time,
the Great Divide community

Stands astride the backbone of the continent,
gathering, draining, reflecting, sending forth
a flow so powerful it seeps rhythmically
from within,

Alive to each of us,
to drink, to swim, to grow corn ears
to listen to our children float the streams
of their own magnificence,

Out of their seeping dreams,
out of their useful silliness,
out of their source-mouths
high and pure,

The Great Divide,
you and I, all that lives
and floats and flies and passes through
all we know of why.

MY LOVE IS LIKE A RIVER

My love is like a river
like a river is to ground
she reaches deep and sweeps to loam
the strength that is the mountains down.

My love is like the seed
that's carried in the air
by wing he picks my hopes to fly
for rooting here and there.

My love is like a rake
with teeth to tame of dreams
the poem a furrowed field makes
row on row she rustles green.

My love is like the grain
that's made the gift of bread
he's the stuff of sustenance
to one who's daily fed.

My love is like a weed
where nothing else will grow
she lights in barren lots and blows
the randy dance of dandelions.

My love is like the wave
when rolling up the sand
in mighty storm of wind and rain
shapes a woman and a man.

HOME

I. *Sweet Home*

Rectangular threshold
lock door window sash

Wire plumb first and second loan
into where

You hang pajamas,
park cars outside of

Only those invited may enter.
Tented thresholds also,

Mountain stream pillow mat
zippered down water bottle

Hike on scree and ruffled papers
into Outlook windows send,

And return

Something there is that wants reprieve
go about in skivvies.

II. *For Which A Warrant Is Necessary*

Consider the magistrate who, with affidavit dangled,
must decide whether to override

Your soiled hamper laundry
hard drive panty memory pantry content.

Sign or refuse to sign? a daily question
only those who love night-silent entry ways

And dawn-lit breakfast nooks should be asked.

III. *To Share*

Hang a lot of hooks and hope another wants to
hang pajamas there

And help you flower sheets.

IV. *Cries*

Whoop-tee-whoop!

Phone rings and all your shrieking's caught
way in the gut and won't let up

Your esophagus enough
for letting go that departing part of you

Not a hinge-on-hinge remaining
Any closure

Admits.

V. *Transports*

Shoes, pants, coat, hat,
flap, configuration

Gesture, spit-upon-the-sidewalk
your dog drools

Jaw-on-paws at the turn-of-your-motor
at the head of your street

Click click click your heel pattern
speaking all your smells

Beloved.

VI. *For What You Give*

And what returns to you,
abides.

COMING INTO FALL

A brooding dark presence
on the Kenoshas stretches horizontally,

Underneath, a band of piled-up clouds,
conjures not-yet snow-bank

Fate of mountains,
they will sleep

But, O! Not-yet,
it's golden aspen's turn to paint

Elk-bugle footprints on foothills
graduating into Fall's

Grade school catechism,
first we taste of all our senses ripening

Then into creation turned out
to find our own ways

Through drought and freeze
unto the Springs that will, that surely will.

THE EDGE OF THINGS

MESA VERDE

Where earth and sky are one
                    we undone
                              have come
                                                  to the edge
                    of things
          and see that spirits dwell
between.

A FOX IN ELDER BERRY RAIN

I would miss the trees
the most, how they talk
when the wind comes up
and bend their backs
for storms to pass,
glisten for return
of shine.

Fishes, too!
I used to count them
best on hook, remove
and fry, then I thought
to put them back, then
to leave them be
And think of streams
they like to dart within,
glistening.

I would
listen more a fox
in elder berry rain
passing in the grass.

LIFT LINES

At timberline where the last
towering trees track the Almighty
in warming huts we wait our turns
to Schuss the Sky.

SIREN

To hear fire women fork
the tongue's own lightning
and, with cracking lips,
say how novice fire men
in a bucket brigade scan
the sky for crackling clouds.

How words can spark and flare,
or lay as smooth as water on
an old man's wrinkled skin,
impart a tangy earthy taste,
or smelling foul of burning flesh
breach a mighty distance

Shrieking speechless fear.
I'd rather call for napalm
on my own position raining down
than to battle demons mute
without her siren verse or song.

SHOULDER STRAP

When mountain peaks
seem so high above
and climbing

Much too difficult
to bear the risk
of bearing up,

Shoulder strap your soul.
Getting there is
feeling that you can.

DEAR FRIEND

Your earth is waking,
I can feel your soil give
to the plant of your heel,
my nostrils swell with the
fragrant smell of your green.
A downslope wind pushes in
from mountain dwellings,
the prairie stirs to welcome
you. And so you go as you
came, dear friend, a blessing!
I shall stay, filled with the joy
of greeting your arrival. Our
meeting will always be where
we started, where the waters
meet to send the waters forth.

OUT THE WINDOW

Some days I look
out the window
and get nothing done
but the looking,
I see the bird lady
feeding pigeons
in Civic Center Park,
I see citizens waving

Multi-colored signs
at the Capitol
or at each other,
I see the naked trees

And when their raiment's full,
growing in the open space
between the monuments,
I see the southern end
of Rocky Mountain Park,
and all the while I dream
of hiking trips
through the streets

To the Confluence,
to Wild Basin,
to Streams
I cannot see.

PRAYER FLAGS

Between elk and hummingbird
descends
intervals of total silence.

You set peanuts out,
and the jays
don't come.

You wonder if the rounded
earth has developed sharp edges
dropping off

The Sirens and the Titans.
You miss all creatures
terribly.

Condition cyclic-temporary?
You must go hanging out
the prayer flags.

CELEBRATE THE CALLERS

Witness the river,
from smaller water
streams

Energy and sweet music,
power of community.
Nature lays the course
men and women
interplay,

Those who listen well
call to others.

TEN POINT AGENDA
FOR THE PUBLIC LANDS

1. Formless
2. Water, land, and air
3. One cells, plants, and creatures
4. Women, men, children
5. Food and shelter
6. Good work
7. Good health
8. Inspiration
9. Community
10. Love.

ENERGY POLICY

On the first day the Lord our God
created an energy policy, he created
the sun, the wind, and the waters.
On the sixth day he created man,
during the eons in between, the earth
the formless wasteland he had parted
from the heavens took shape, plants
and creatures coming and going stored
in faults and aquifers the sun they had
borrowed, and the wind blew constantly.

When appeared the men and the women,
they inhabited the arc of the sun by day,
and struck by night, from rock and tinder,
holy fire to cook and light and warm
whatever hours fell between, and the
wind blew constantly. From the spark
the intellect he had given them, the men
and the women forged wondrous implements
for converting the insurance stored in the earth
into power and particles, and they began to

Turn their habitations away from the sun,
and the new gods on the sixth day
said, "It is good!" And the wind
blew constantly.

GOOD COLORADO
HEADWATERS EDUCATION

Good we don't have to buy the weather,
good isn't for sale and just happens whenever.
Predictions, though good and getting better,
are wildly inaccurate when the best worst weather
hits so suddenly you can't tell where the pitch
comes from.

I prefer weather to politics,
I mean, at least, when you sear your lips
or an will wind spanks your bottom, you can
rightly say, "Wait a minute, it'll change"—
Colorado axiom, any politics charging straight
off the Divide is worth standing to for.

Sure you have to hunker down when thunder
booms and lightning catches between a vortex
pit-of-gut instinct and a gearing rain that may never
touch ground. "Norm" is only a mathematical
Possibility. Yell, "Hail!" and run. Your average-
staked tent blows down any minute.

THE HYDROLOGIC CYCLE

Sea to the river
Feed me

River to the aquifer
Fill me

Aquifer to the earth
Hold me

Earth to the clouds
Seed me

Clouds to the wind
Stir me

Wind to the sea
Rinse me

Earth to the aquifer
Aquifer to the river
River to the sea
Sea to the wind
Wind to the clouds
Clouds to the earth

Seed me
Stir me
Rinse me
Feed me
Fill me
Hold me.

BETSY'S WINDOW

You of the fingering brushes coaxing
light from depths of overwhelming shade, to
ooze the shape and source of origins, jug
or water from the jug, or she who holds
and tips fresh clay for ovening's touch, can
you tell me, O dear Troubadour, of flame's
first history, and you biographer
of Abelard, what sing of Heloise,
her form, or fire in the forms of two of
them igniting when first a thermal popped
from whence? (But, Ah! The Wonder) a thermal's
hatched, between pigments and layers of torches.
Out through Betsy's window swells a green sea
and plein air artists wake stretching pancakes.

RAINBOWS

Rainbows fade the closer we get to them,
greens and reds move into violets, mist
pervades, the slanting sun cuts
in and out, our faces drip dew,
we feel treasured.

GALADRIEL'S MIRROR

At the end
when sullen thunder and the rain begins
to sleeve a farther peak
or two,
signs portend a trusted friend will know
the lightest way to go;

She cinches down a Kelty pack and fits
my poncho for a walk
as when we started leaving years ago,
between the pauses and the talk
in fun we've lent the sun a spark
or two
for storing up;

Then she sets this Hobbit loose
upon the wind
that wafts the peaks from Lórien.

SPRING

Ache for knowing
snow is really gone,
though it goes
in daffodils.

Have a life worth having,
fish O!
a thousand streams,
no sense quibbling,
Spring has come again.

WEATHERING

When
I've seen enough
of blue or gray or golden skies

and felt sufficient wind
for remembering
all its different touchings

and seasons' turn
has turned me in
I'll take shelter from this living

Until then I'm content
to weather
each beginning.

IF I COULD CHOOSE

If I could choose where I'd be eternally?
I'd rather be a mountain stream
or bury me deep in canyon country.

MADE FOR BLUE

Clouds curtain peaks.

Though clear on through the pass
a scratch of blue
our topo maps are wearing thin
and indistinguishable.

Evening storm is bearing in
and we've not yet pitched camp
or made for blue.

PARADISE?

Are mountains high in paradise?
Do streams run crystal clear?
Can I meet my lady there?
Will we lay face up in wildflowers?

Shall we hold ourselves in paradise
as we do each other here?

Has the sky a million stars?

AUGUST NATION

August should be burning, is it feigning
lightning polls that open up the heavens?
Got the sprinklers turned to off, let it rain!

Thunder's in the meadow, and its gaining
ground. Come on down! Come on down! Yo-Leaven!
August should be burning what is feigning.

Sow weather for a change must have a brain
crop soil moisture needs-or else be riven-
got off the sprinklers turned to let it rain.

Roll up the meadow hay twelve crickets claim,
bridle up the brindled ponies given
and August burning should not-be-feigning

Pipe the pipers here, name them by their names:
Gramps, MaMa, baby Jose Finnegan
got sprinklers turning off, so let them rain!

A Nation's only people, all remains
for choosing how their best can grace be gained.
August should be burning, is it feigning?
Got the sprinklers turned to off, let it rain!

URBAN WILD PERCHES

THE OWLS ARE BACK!

The owls are back!
Owl weather brings them in,
feathering owling rain.
When the sun finally
levers the cloud through
the boughs, the blue
spruce by the alley couches
them. On tip toes neighbors
Slide along the neighboring
walls, whispering, "The owls
Are back! The owls are
Back!" and shut up the
Dogs. Owls are evil,
owls are wise, owls are
mysterious, our owls
fly into urban wild perches
we long them to visit.

CIVIL ENGINEERS

Civil engineers and fishermen
practice line drawing and line arcing
over rivers and into pools.

Where place the struts
to bear the weight
of a crossing?

Where place the lure
to attract wild forces
inter-playing?

Where stresses meet
pushing and pulling
to the counter-balancing.

VERIFY

I often wonder how
on a flat surface the
Artist can display
how cliffs hang from
the air. I touch
the gorge for a clue
and verify no rocks
or river. I stand back.
Light plays on the upper
lips of the precipice.

INVOCATION

Lord,
we interplay in your fields,
sometimes faithfully, somewhat fitfully.
All spaces connect us, vast space we look
up to when wonder overtakes our nights,
singing fish wrapped in meandering
ribbons murmuring through our hearts.

Lord,
may we honor those among us who
argue strongly for the strength of
understanding, who have understood
their limits and do not cease a passage
through, who substitute the opportunity
they have for the opportunity they pass along.

Lord,
help us turn our advocacy to the good
of community, to look past what we
think others are doing to us
to what we can do together on this
Earth, in this time we have to treasure.

Bless this good company.

SOME SNOW

Some snow is so light
will seem to pull the sleeping
ash and cherry up,

Other snow is malicious—
cracks a branch, no difference
young or old.

Though this heavy kind of snow
is best for reservoirs
and snowmen,

The lighter kind delights
a quiet cup of coffee or
walk around the block.

YOUR VOICE ARRIVED

I must tell you, friend,
my heart gladdened
when your voice
arrived with snow
and rivers and those
stars hiding within,
above, behind the ice
fog. In that place
where burning fierce
and bright they blaze on,
whether or not I
can see them.

POWERFUL VERSIONS

The great king Ramses
on his funerary
arranged

For the sun to shine on his face
mid-February,
his birthday.

Here come the spikes of the yellow crocus
years ago
I planted for us

Where you asked me to.
Please, these lovely peach roses from Ecuador,
maybe Cuenca?

Walking together
the river walk.

I LIKE THE FEEL OF A BOOK

I like the feel of a book,
the way it cradles in your palm
and peels open to thumb
and forefinger, I like turning
leaves, on every leaf engrained
by some creator, a story of
discovery, I would dwell in a
forest of leaves, way up
in the canopy, to see the river
traders pass below with coconut
and crocodilians, or along the
route of caravans, perch in
a lone acacia tree to spy
a sway of camels conveying
silk to Byzantium, and why spiders
have so many eyes. I should like
to hear the troubadours sing of
lost and gallant warriors falling
in the train of Charlemagne or
sailing off beyond the Hesperides,
and how to tie a caddis fly
and set it gently down upon
the spine of rising waters.

APRIL COLD FRONT

Under the cruel
weight of an April
cold front,
low against the
huddled earth wet
with tears,
seared by drought
and locust prophecy,
waits the strong
and delicate star-
shaped columbine.

OLD FRIEND

Old Friend,

I've seen you since a sprout,
a shoot, a sapling, a stupendous
white flower bee-gathering offering,

By-early-July your abundant red and
sour delicious manifest drooping full
and staggering in the ripe of the bearing-up,

Then would all the urban wild creatures
flock-run-gobble-grab what you held-
to-glory out to them, so graciously.

Not fair, not fair, not fair!
My fair and failing ailing one,
crippled by the axe-wielding

Fell-blow of Not-Quite-Spring
standing once-again on the verge
of all your Pilgrim-to-Prairie finery,

Smacking to the heart-core your standing-forth—
you the catch-dew, you the cuneiform, you who cup
the pitch-berries of each and every possibility.

I will pray. I will work. I will string a web of those
not-forgetting struts for the propping-up, that
you, Old Friend, may revisit time-and-again.

A PERFECT HALO

A perfect halo surrounds the moon
Early March night, though a large slice
Icing down from right to left across
The diagonal creates a dark half.

This halo's brightest at the center, radiating
Lesser light to an encircling rose/violet band.
Rumble off a passing train roughs up the lower Platte,
Downtown Monday morning shakes towards Daylight.

CHANNELS

Thunder calls, your grandson
hears the rumble, runs to the door
front you had bolted from the chill
last November, and pulls you through.
Another flash charges the hinge
between the two of you, you hold
hands waiting for the next clap,
you could explain how clouds
assume this responsibility.
Cherry blossoms shake loose,
somewhere a turtle periscopes
her head between her doors
and looks around, worms feel
the pattern of the falling clouds.
Robins and farmers hope,
channels swell.

MANY RIVERS

Many rivers flow from the mountains,
all would head for the sea, I hear
your tributary bubbling. Mine
takes joy in knowing your
flow also takes shape in the
struggle that shapes making
its own way off the mountain.

ELLIPSE

South side of the ellipse
in the heart of the city—
interposed between local
and state courts—art museum
and the public library.

On the east axis, the golden
dome of the capitol-dipped
in dawn, glowing sentinel to
a westering sky—looks to the
heart of the Continent.

Round the north curvature,
the press and downtown businesses—
commerce and the stuff of daily
commentary—offset history,
culture, with contemporaries.

The people come and go
across their park at the center,
gather and retreat along diagonals,
the People's Fair, Festival of
Mountains, Festival of Plains.

Every step they take, here history,
here art, here business, here
government, here the common
space—
here the future, here the past.
Always present, always different.

COTTONWOOD

On the plains
nearly every tree's been planted
but the cottonwood.
It siphons up the seeps and
spreads to green every drop
that happens through the dust
and ice. You can wander in
the streets that happened to
these plains, and never believe one.
Though an irrigated forest may
temper those who dwell beneath,
you must root along a lowly creek
tucked within the Urban Flood
Control and Drainage District
to practice such a lonely free and
independent creed.

ONE BODY, ONE SPIRIT, MANY FUTURES

Those who came before—yes,
they are with us still.
We know them by their names:
Need, Conflict, Confusion, Good
Will. They made—as best they could—
a compact, a basic apportionment,
based on the lay of the land
and the need of the people.

The idea is this: fifty-fifty,
the upper, the lower, head-to-toe,
joined at the gut and the hip—
mountains, the great Grand Canyon,
the vast Southwest—always
the River at the heart of all
possibility. And, so, we go
one body, one spirit, many futures.

MS. DUSTY MILLER

Ms. Dusty Miller,
you've flown from Kansas
to rattle at the light
inside my lampshade
at the head of this reading couch,

So you might continue
I've left the back door open
to the mountains,
but you prefer Edison
to the Exit

And I'll not mind
your wings punctuating
this page of May's ending

Pre-dawn.

I AM A WESTERN PERSON

I am a Western person
educated to yellow cactus
flowers and snow
white peaks,

California to Colorado,
Alaska to New Mexico,
shaped for beneficial use
born to a higher purpose,

We are visitors,
lifetime visitors,
shaped for beneficial use
born to a higher purpose.

WE CALL IT THE END OF THE DAY

We call it the end of the day,
black squirrels have cracked
the last sunflower seed,
alone, a doe, high steps her
way through the sweet grass,
lavender paints the underbelly
of a Rocky Mountain whaling
ship, part of a fleet bound
for the Divide, blue waves recede
hill on hill, but we…fare in.

INVOCATION II

Lord,

Bless like water flowing all persons assembled here,
Bless the land that sustains and inspires us,

Bless each other and every form of life we share the world with, Bless all
the elements and the composite of all the elements,

Like water drawn from a natural spring or lake, river or well,
All the works of intellect,
All the works of common sense and practicality,

Joy of work, Separation from work,
Joy of community, Separation from community,

Time to engage, Time to reflect, Time to re-engage,

Love of family, Love of neighbor, Love of friend, Love of colleague,
Love of each with whom we disagree,

Lord,

Help us see the good in everyone and everything, Help us to recall:
That no award or recognition we bestow or receive is other than
recognition of contribution to community,

That there is no opportunity but the opportunity others have provided
us, and the opportunity we provide to others,

That true pride in the good that each of us accomplishes is born of true
humility springing, welling, flowing from your nurturing grace.

THE STORY

The story is the power
Of the Teacher. Seated round
A circle chalked, children loose
Bright canoes their tether cords,
Currents take them. Unto the morning
Mist, graceful diving birds are launched.
Fierce orchids hang fragrant. Cooking smokes
Curl up, River Traders pass. Wider twice
Than craft, prehistoric fishes glide.
Fernlike trees are filled with
Howling forms. These little
Ships, the Wilderness,
Are deftly held.
Her Voice
Eddies
On.

POLIS

"Polis" is an ancient word for self-governed community.

The Greek City State,
the Greeley Colony,

Family, girl or boy scout troop, farm lot, schoolroom, athletic field, feed
lot, bank board, water board, trout pool, the open range,
plains or mountain campfire.
A time and place for gathering round a source of light and warmth
and dinner sizzle-cooked of fish filet or rib aroma on the wind,

For gathering round the bard, the story-teller, the gentle politician—
motivator, statesman, prophet—
he or she who stirs glowing embers for the sparks to rise,
as though ascending fireflies

Are winging to all degrees and possibilities
a compass may point to.

Ideas born of campfires are glimmering fireflies,
to stir them really good for wing-taking takes some really good
heartwood, a firm and kindly touch, visions that stir in the heart
so to part the dark, so they might see on through the shadows
confidently—whoever's heart you might touch. It takes politic.

"Politic" means shrewd and prudent, tactful and diplomatic.
teacher, mentor, guide, truth-sayer, father, son, grandson,
husband, grandfather—W.D.
your initials mean, "We'll do."

For you have said there's no one else
to do the job as well as each of us will do together.
'S true, W.D., You're you. But you're also the land, the water, the shining
mountains, the lamb, the talking raven, limb of spruce,
limb of cottonwood.

You have loved Colorado as much
as any man or woman, in a lifetime,
can. To tell a truth
you love this time, this place,
these people, these rivers singing,
this Colorado—
lakes in their depths, the sound of a headgate opening, the
gurgling, the running of the laterals to the rustling corn,

Joy of the harvest, of commerce, of self-formed men and women,
of the nurturing of kids,
of the voice of your soul's companion, Judy,
she who traveled with you from passage to vista
and through the ordinary moments of the ordinary moments,

Isn't this—the each and all of this—
what you've been telling us around the campfire?
"Stand firm when needed, always hear the wisdom of
another's point of view, when right or resolving grace

Demand, accommodate,"
to believe that we can let fly the sparks of community?

Now, W.D.,
you have brought us food and water,
insight of substance seen—and seldom seen—
in decades yet to come from all that's come before

Take to heart this branding iron,

This symbol of the mark we bear of you
you have sealed, in our hearts and minds, the initials "W.D."
They mean "wide distance." Far countries
as close as the nearest neighbor, as distant as the plan
we make tomorrow, as wide as the many hands
of citizens
to whom you would have us consign the future
for safekeeping.

(Presentation for W.D. Farr, Citizen of the West Award)

LIGHT HURTS

A FEW SLENDER NEEDLES

Pulling slow at first,
as though uncertain
a few slender needles
could hold her up,
the moon gigantic
chins her way
needle-by-needle,
limb-by-limb to the
crown, then balancing
on the topmost rung,
pauses to say farewell
to August, then moves on.

HEAR THE CRICKET

I distinctly hear the cricket
inside the house
behind the couch where the dog
with ears cocked;

Feel a cold damp coming in,
turn more lights on,
unpile a downy quilt,
fire the furnace up.

Call my Mom.

LORD, HELP US

Lord, help us understand
what we cannot know for sure,
every day's a gift,

Every evening an opportunity,
to practice grace and thankfulness,
to place our faith in community,

For all we have, for all the nows
and now, is the chance
of being, day and evening,

Together and alone,
to walk the shore and mountain path,
to lift our voices,

Work for peace,
honor hope,
love greatly.

THE DAY THE MOUNTAINS SCREAM

An ordinary day half a continent away,
oakbrush and aspen burn gold and scarlet,
streams are lower and clearer, native trout
settle below rocks to catch a nymph or
hellgrammite. But bears are desperate,
they roam for food and scratch for dreams,
the day the mountains scream.

An ordinary day half a continent away,
breakfast coffee and conversation,
goodbye to family, the morning newspaper,
a subway ride, another cup of coffee,
hello to colleagues, booting up, checking
messages, making plans for client lunch,
the day the mountains scream.

An ordinary day half a continent away,
Lewis writes in his journal, marks fresh charts,
hunters set out, other men point the tips
of their long poles West and push upstream,
a native woman, her French husband guide them,
pilgrims follow, churches, schools, the Grange,
the day the mountains scream.

An ordinary day half a continent away,
Moses, Muhammed, Christ, Siddartha,
Confucius, take up their walking staffs,
into the hills, into the valleys, into the
poisoned wells of the most hardened
hearts, the peoples walk with them,
the day the mountains scream.

An ordinary day half a continent away,
the eagle and the raven land on peaks
and city streets, Daedalus and Icarus
strap on their wings and launch, they
do not know if air shall carry them,

they only dare to feel it will some day,
the day the mountains scream.

The day the mountains scream
is just an ordinary day, we wake,
we sleep, we work, we play, we
dance, we scheme, we fight, we
blame, we weep, we pray, we ask
forgiveness, we forgive, we bless
an ordinary day half a continent away.

SPLIT ROCK

Just when you think the country
desolate, a sweet creek bubbles up,
grasses sprout, what you left behind
can stay there, air is snappier here,
light hurts you can see by.

A SCIENCE LESSON

It wasn't even a stream
it was an irrigating ditch
near the end of its season,
tall shocks shorn, too early
yet for snow geese. Our
Granddaughter hands us
each a rock, hers a third,
leads us to the center
of the bridge. We look over
The cut. "You throw yours
First!" she instructs her
Grandmother, and runs to
the opposite side. To spot
the rock floating under
The bridge. She waits,
then runs back to me,
"You try now," she urges.

RAINING OWLS

Out here it rains owls,
great horned and barn,
when hail falls as big
as fists, rips corn from
shrouds and only stalks
stand exactly where
they were. Windows
fly in, roofs disintegrate.
When it rains owls
coyotes stutter, ground
in July looks January,
whirlwind descends
angry-pit of angry-gut

hurling bit of angry
dust, bits of angry
rain against the other.
Hurling them again-
and-again against
the upper atmosphere,
until the bottom falls
utterly outside in.

INDIAN SUMMER

A searing frost, then the green and golden
grip simmers, waiting, waiting, for the core.
Blue, the truer mountains become bluer,
streams concentrate, lower, clearer, pooling
those who depend upon wet nourishing—
letters, numbers, relationships, stories,
speaking, reading, reflecting, sharing joy,
ingathering, underfoot dry grasses,
Crunch! You cubs, you fawns, prepare
yourselves well. Eat, browse, drink,
snort, shake your fur, stretch your skin.

LOVE'S RETURN

I've not missed you~
Much~
Not much more~
Than a lung
      Under water~
 Misses air

Or the sea run~
Steelhead~
Not much more~
Than a nook
      He came~
From

Oh~
I've not missed you~
Much~
Not much more
      Than robin's~
Food

Or the star run~
Night~
Misses gleaming~
Than a sprung
      Upwelling~
Artesian

I've not missed you~
Much~
Not much more~
Than a lip
      Alone~
Misses.

ROCK THAT WEARS

Our friendship
like the rock
that wears the waterfall
roars and sings
through the pounding
and the seeping seasons.

SWEET SUMMER SOLSTICE

Sweet summer solstice,
you lick the nape of our necks
with the cool tongue of your long
evening light, peeling back the night
to fill the peaches we shall savor
when nights grow fuller.

SKINS

September's skin is green,
October golden,
November olive,

As a young girl
turns to teen
then to woman,

Tones of expectation,
tones of experience,
turn from within,

Feeling, breathing,
touching, protecting,
embracing, sloughing,

Hues of trimming
tides, many
many moons.

MAD WITH THE MOON

Through the stratocirrus clouds
the haloed moon bursts over
the edge of the world across
the eastern plains. It does
not exist to serve, yet it does.

I put on my hiking boots, my
snow shoes, my cross country
skies, my running shoes, my
cowboy boots, my go-about-
the-circumference night slippers.

I leap. O wall, O earth, O universe!
I see your island face floating,
shining in the seas, every space
entire to the other. I love you as
a lover will, mad with the moon.

MONET'S WATER GARDEN

Lilies
dip their wings
in clouds,

Cloistered
willows pray
Matins,

Purple choirs
sing praise to
no other Light.

WELCOME, RAIN!

Drip the gutters and the brick,
Drip the benches and the deck,
Drip the sidewalks and the street,
Drip the pathways and the park,
Drip the blossoms and the leaf,
Drip the grasses and the root,
Drip the pages and the book.

WHITE MOTHS, YELLOW BUTTERFLIES

White moths, yellow butterflies,
wall flower, sulphur flower, golden
banner wing petals fluttering
in June aftermath of battle drum
thunder squalls, mountain mid-
afternoon summer precursors.

KEYSTONE AGREEMENT

Loveland Pass to the Sea
of Cortez, in between some
of the finest, loneliest, most
bizarre, peaceful, roiled,
spoiled, tamed, wild, beguiling,
salty, plain, mundane, beautiful,
unexplained people
the lizards, aspen, condors,
cougar, snakes, cutthroat,
raven, scorpions, cows,
willows, coyote, chub, elk,
mesa, bison, falls, sheep,
canyon, rim, pinnacles, wren,
coral, delta, river, peaks
have ever seen.

THE DIFFERENCE BETWEEN A DUCK

A duck don't know the difference
between jurisdictional waters
and a pothole, if there's water
he'll land. Sometimes the law
don't know the difference
between a duck.

HYDROPATHIC THERAPY

Hydropathic therapy n : of or pertaining to the curative or medicinal power of water: 1: hot springs, e.g., Glenwood, Idaho, Manitou, Ouray, Pagosa, Princeton, first used by Native Americans, rediscovered by nineteenth century tuberculins 2: spas: a: mountain resorts catering to salubrious qualities: b: device of spouting jets capable of installation in any human habitation 3: living waters, by immersion or droplets sprinkled on the forehead~men, women, children

INHERITANCE

Earth will dress itself
layer on layer with garments
cut for future revelation,
custom, dress, and speech.
And none shall ever speak
with such authority as mountains
and the rivers do with sediment.
Whomsoever piñons gather shall
inherit.

ENERGY

Energy of rain,
Energy of seas,
Energy of rivers
Running to the sea.

Energy of you,
Energy of me,
Energy of peoples'
Unique geographies.

Energy of seed,
Energy of loam,
Energy of sprouts
Breaking through their shrouds.

Energy of light,
Energy of dark,
Energy of voyaging
Land and sea and sky.

WHAT I LIKE ABOUT CHEESMAN RESERVOIR

Taking my son-in-law and grandson there,
seeing families fish the in-between zone
where nothing bites but the brilliant blue
of a mountain sky in May and the ever-
changing wind, skipping stones across
the water, thundering contrast the
South Platte makes beneath a
high masonry wall to escape.

THE ICE MACHINE

, a stream feeds in
through a system of gates canals pipes
beneath the streets
beneath the mall buses
beneath the 19th and 21st centuries
and the century
of never ending ways to make war
and wilderness shrink

, a system of laws mostly invented
mostly to get across another man's property
rates charges counter-charges about the stream
being dried up or not
constantly dig up the streets
to put the latest device to put the stream here
sometimes wait for another pipe to burst
from serving tenants of these streets

, whose names go overseas Cuba France Saipan Korea Afghanistan
to fight whose right it might be to take
what the snows have given
make it into feces and urine
gurgle through the tubing
whir the cubes felling into a slot
to be born to glasses stirred swallowed emptied
back to the stream.

RIVER WITHOUT WATER

River without water,
humans without faith.
Faith moves mountains closer
and plains as far as hearts
can see. A flute, a drum,
the thrum of bees in ponderosa,
thump of multi-colored woodpecker,
crack of clouds making electricity,
we come into this country pilgrims
across a land bridge, a sea bridge,
a bridge of air. We come into this
country expecting better of ourselves
than other places we could be—
buildings, roads, dams, power
lines hold and carry only
our temporary.

BEING OF RIVERS FLOWING

Where blinding sundown breaks
into russet couches and bean bag chairs
scatter in the endless sky,

Always the sky,
awake, asleep,
in raucous disposition,
pit of night or streaking gray,

Deepest hue of Mountain Ute,
mud brown of cliff houses,
boundless blue of swirling streams

Fitting place for dinosaurs
roaming where an old sea's
been lifted up
to cave-pocked rimrock

Towering mountain top
the hard way up
in cold wind
on talus rock

Dunes as on oceans,
valleys like bays,
pine tree canopies,

Eagles, woodrats,
porphyry,
being of rivers
flowing,

Colorado.

WHICH COLORADO SHALL WE BE?

I wander through a state that's grown
from out of prairie grass, a state of roots
in confluence of creek and river path.
I loathe this state, I love this state, for what
it's been and is, mean and dusty, lovely, green,
which Colorado shall we be?

I'm the state of Chivington, of hounding out Chinese,
of walking through the streets in sheets and
fixing school boundaries to keep them Afros out.
I'm the state of parks and trees, of getting exercise,
of welcome you, I'd like to help, what interests you,
which Colorado shall we be?

TO A FRIEND WHO WOULD BE SECRETARY OF INTERIOR

Lewis and Clark didn't really know where
they were going, they had a vacant
map and reports of wondrous geography.
They said to each other at the outset
"Let's go on together, there is no other
I'd rather share the journey with!"

They got prepared for what they didn't
know, how to keep their eyes open
and love the land they were passing
through and every living thing they saw.
They took what they needed to survive
and left the rest untouched, knowing

Others would stop where they had pushed
On—and had a needless fight with a bear.

SETTING OUT

LABYRINTH

You may go,
though you do not
know the way,

You see imperfectly
your face in the waters,
wavering.

You are incomplete,
your feet the shape
of they,

But your toes
are curled to a
different direction.

You carry few
accoutrements,
wit, reason, passion,

Traveling companions,
the morning star,
a labyrinth.

Power to engage
connections, deduce
choices, enjoy commitment,

Pick a place
of entry, you can
amaze.

The way will
wind back on
itself,

Lead away from
the center.
Inevitably

You will find
yourself
in the middle,

All directions
surround your
surprise.

ON BEING SWORN

I can help you with your pack,
you can help me, too

We've each a mighty load to carry on,
there's lots of fishing left to do.

Don't forget the meadow frisbee
and the cards for Hearts and War,

We'll switch the lead from time
to time, when I might lag

And you're all speed. Guess I ought
to say it now, before we start to

Strain and sweat, the view ahead
is what we'll earn and not

A finer day for hiking through.

THE GREAT OUTDOOR COLORADO TRUST

You work with what we love the best,
the land, the air, the water, the creatures,
each other. You work with Colorado.

May you love our rivers well, help
us walk along them! Mountains, valleys,
hills and mesas, elk and raven,

Trout, frog and cricket, cities that
hold our spirits to work and play.
Our best, may you help us see

And hear them well, to live among them,
to use what we need beneficially,
to leave as much alone as we have loved

From the borders of the plains
to the glories of the canyons
unto the Great Divide.

DRIFT OF AN UPSLOPE WIND

I compose opinions
with my back to the capitol
and my eyes towards Long's Peak,
through a tunnel of buildings
I look to the Great Divide.

I imagine tipis
at the confluence, cottonwoods,
unbridled ponies dipping nuzzles
into prairie stream and mountain
stream.

I call upon the ribs
of wagons and the ribs of men
and women who lie beneath these
streets, stretching from here
to Golden.

I hear them reassembling
creaking and murmuring, their
voices the leaves turning turning,
drift of an upslope wind between
my fingers.

YOU BUY THE BACKPACK

You buy the backpack
or the suitcase
expecting adventure,

But never knowing whether.
You may plan on wine-soaked
mussels at Collioure,

Or stew a la Dinty Moore
atop a San Juan mountain pass,
whether you enjoy the food,

Or eat to survive the trip,
is incapable of prior resolution.
To resolve in the setting out

To be resolute in the journeying
is to savor unexpected dishes
through every kind of weather.

HOW JOURNEYS BEGIN

Loving lady
faithful dog
hardy pair of boots

As close to comfort
as a man can stand
his ground with

Finding the right fit
for feet and feelings

How journeys
and civilization begin
the mind a step at a time

Without complaint
or need of moleskin.

RIGHT EQUIPMENT

The urban west is gaining on the rural,
eighty-five percent of us can't see Orion.

"Unless we go camping," said my tent.
"Glad you broke me in," said my hiking boots.

"Thirty-six percent of Colorado
Is public land," said my backpack.

Thank God for right equipment.

MY TENT

My tent's never met a mountain it didn't like.
it hates being in a bag, tells me so mid-winter.

Not St. Mary's glacier again, I pray!
"Anywhere, you say, my friend. Just let me out!"

I take to staking out, frame and canopy,
a place above.

BACKPACKING

Backpacking is Skill,
Art, Means
of Survival—

Whether in Wilderness
or Therapy,
placing Proper

Food, Clothing
in Water-Tight bags—
together with a First Aid Kit

And Pocket Knife
only then require
a Good Guide—

Family, Friends,
True Map and
Compass.

SLIPSTREAM

Finding much comfort in
tail races, fresh water,
and steady mealtimes,
I am a hatchery fish

Launched from the back
of a truck. Totally wild
and wily trout swimming
by my frantic bubbles,

Flipping madly, I manage
to fit into the slipstream
behind the lead swimmer.
I say, "How do you do

That?" "Laugh a lot!"
he grins. I also notice
he gets in early, stays
late, and always resists

Plunging straight ahead
whenever someone pokes
a wearied gill into his pool
for guidance. One day

He swims the waterfall,
leaving us to paddle on
with the hatchery trout
tucked in our slipstreams.

THANKS FOR TRAVELING

Thanks for traveling with me awhile,
I've enjoyed your company. I'm grateful
you saw differently enough the same
Geography. I'd be looking at the ground,
you'd be looking through the trees for
land forms, then we'd switch positions
to argue a better way at junction
trails. Now, you're off in another
direction, may the bond we've formed
in the joy of journeying lead you on.

MAY I TELL YOU

May I tell you this?
When I love you my skin
stretches from head to heel,
rivers run through tunnels
that lead me to you.

I am renewed, I hope you too,
I can never be alone when I am
alone with you. May we call these
moments of intense creativity
prayer, and pray often?

For we have been given to share
in all that is divine. None of the telling
alone could have told me this, what your
heart and tongue will tell. What stories
we speak by loving!

FELLOW SWIMMER

In my judicial writing,
I try to focus on what
I am sentencing
The reader to,

When I attempt the prose
or stanza poem,
I switch from plain
to metaphor

To swim against the riptide,
one ear cocked to the
solitary, the other for
the Secret Sharer.

OXBOWS

I love everything water has to do with,
plants, fish, frogs, birds, people,
how they come to be independent,
interdependently,

I love the way unique rivers bend
goosenecks back on themselves,
hello, nice seeing you, goodbye!
Geese flying over.

Cole and his oxbow glowing
East to West, muleback, wagon
back, horseback, foot tracks
between the watering holes,

Will we make it? Maybe not.
Got to find out! While that glow
is glowing back and waters flow,
trickle, disappear—you and me.

PEBBLES

The sea will empty pebbles into your
pocket, empty your pockets and let the
sea in. Pock-smooth and rounded black and white
rosey-shaped pebbles sneak unexpected
seams. You dry out and find them, unnoticed.

THE FIRST APPLE BLOSSOMS

The first apple blossoms after a big storm
are the sweetest.

The fester-cluster that forced the question
before the answers—

Unfolded, what about the dry, the hidden,
? What if.

Dissolved in the soaking
snow crystals, leach understanding—
We lack patience with patience, what seems
often, never is

And we are left with. . . . what is.
The destruction we seed never is

Equal to the twig that holds the ascending
cascade we can't blame,

Or confuse with anything we are responsible
for creating.

CALIBRATING THE MODEL

What question are you trying to answer?

Here's the code,
there never will be
or can be
a perfect outcome . . .
and, yet, a method.

Boundaries must be set
along the mountain front,
Darcy's law,
the inflow and the outflow
need to balance,

In between's the stress,
the driving force
that brings about all
the gaining and the losing reaches,
all the small—and great—

Connections.
Collect the data,
find a map,
make a history,
make a wish . . .

Then go figure!
Gravity and density
are features of the earth
men and women
have the opportunity to emulate—

Geometry, slope of the channel,
fractures, moisture content.
There never will
or can be
a perfect outcome...

Yet, a robust and respectful direction,
a stratigraphy of learning
and participating we may all
contribute to the flow,
despite every uncertainty.

CALIFORNIA WATER

California water starts in the heart
of the Sierra and the Rockies, in
Oregon north of the Lassen country,
up in the mother lode of snow.
So many rivers, so much beauty,
land of the Golden Trout and
the Monterey Bay fandango,
a place where many peoples sail

To where the rails begin to intercept
a nation made of so many nations,
its water law reflects a polyglot
of doctrine—continuous flow and the
mining camp, of pump whenever you
can and leave it alone to shape
the fish and the land—where Delta
and Omega tap the Range of Light

And nobodies out of Oklahoma and
China lent their muscle and were
spat at. It's a wonder the way golden
poppies and the sea otter dance
upon the hills, in the waving kelp forest,
and the remnant Giant Sequoia still
hold their chance to keep on standing
depends, really depends, doesn't it?

FARMING FOR BIRDS

The improbable Sally Shanks of Staten Island—
far from the Eastern Shore, this is the California Bay Delta
Staten Island—farms for birds, cows, and humans,
corn, wheat, and tomatoes.

Ibis, trumpeters, sand hill cranes delight in Sally's place,
taking off and crying out, they tuck their prehistoric toes
behind a set of sleek and lovely wings, hooting
Sally's contemporary into the next field.

Improbable, the means and pattern of irrigation, too.
Levees make the island whole and possible, Sally lets
the water in for standing birds to feed, pumps
the water out to grow the crops.

Just over there, the Sacramento ship channel, down
the line a massive set of pumps to take the water south
to other farms, many people. Salmon get confused
about which the Sacramento, where the

San Joaquin? The place isn't what it used to be
for anyone or anything—California, I mean—so improbable
to a purpose, Sally and her crew of worker-birds
muck and call for Re-Beginnings.

BEAM-DRIFT

Before I go to bed, a ringing in
my ears sounds me of the coming din
when I will hear nothing but the ringing.

A road across a water path the moon
makes for traveling along when next she
needs a path to walk across the waters.

And I will take that road some night alone,
me, a buoy, and the moon walking up
that thread of light treading on some beam-drift.

THE FIREHOLE RIVER

Steam rises from the rift
of the Firehole River,
a blizzard rages.

Leave your icy pants
and shoes, slip over
the lips

Of the Firehole River
into the murmuring
Mist. Persist,

You'll need no face
to hang in this place
of the thermal

Subterraneans,
only the drift of the
Firehole River

Voices bubbling through
from ancient France,
China, Madagascar,

Say something, let it go.

FIRE & DROUGHT

CUP A MATCH

When hiking in the mountains,
you can camp a fire
and wait out the storm,
or wade into it,

Anger is blind,
stirs the wind,
can't read a map
or cup a match.

GOING TO GUNNISON

Going to Gunnison,
mist of burning embers
from the Hi Meadow
South Platte wildfire,
foal romping in a field,
lady strapping on her hiking boots
for a day on Mt. Sherman,
Arkansas River flowing
towards the Bessemer,
4 Corners Rafting,
valley of the Gunnison,
three working dogs on a hay truck,
Western State College,
we are educated in community
everywhere beauty instructs us.

DROUGHT

West slope peaches are ripening
smaller and faster. We put seed
and water out hoping to alleviate
drought's suffering in the perimeter
we can affect. Swooping gait
of chickadees descends shrilling
of bounty found, steller jay
and downy woodpecker follow
on. Country squirrels abide their
ground, daring our city dog who
is content to lounge away her
lame and lengthening afternoon.
Hornets attend hummingbird
feeders as barflies do a football
game, frantic for honey water.
Red fox will show by evening,
But I . . . I must depart.

THE GREAT UNCONFORMITY

Between a sill and rift of zoroaster granite
clings the tamarisk and barrel cactus,
desert bighorn sheep, between them a third,
kid-sized. A flock of snowy egrets skims
the Continental Drift. Worm and reptile
tracks are common, lungfish, crocodilians,
willow twig replicas, cobbled, uplifted.
The River, sinuous, follows no fault system
faithfully, it breaks topographic obstacles.
Back-swimmers, water-striders, we stretch our
deformation to join the absent ancient ones
of the Great Unconformity.

YIELD

Fields, grasses, woods and hills, hold you closely.
From all we used to be, every void and
particle, moisture, mineral, unique
double curving binding twist unwinding,
we offer up and yield.

Our names on stones
inscribed shall sink and fall unreadable,
all churches shall be converted to song.
Springs shall bubble up, reappear the fields,
grasses, woods and hills. Offer up and yield

From all we used to be, shall every void and fill.

WELL I NEVER BEEN TO NINEVEH

Well, I never been to Nineveh,
Can't even spell its name,
But I been to Lo Do Denver
And, man, they got some sinners there!

God, he says to Jonah, tell them I am mad,
Gonna' send my fire down ! ! !
And gonna' burn/ and gonna' burn/
And gonna' burn IT to the ground!

Holy smoke!   Says Jonah,
I'm hangin' up the phone,
Get me off your call list now!
I got no dog in this.

Well, I never been to Nineveh,
Can't even spell its name,
But I been to Lo Do Denver
And, man, they got some sinners there!

The Lord, he sends a Fish,
The biggest Fish you ever saw,
And makes that Fish go swallow up
That no-good, VERY reluctant Prophet.

The Fish, she does a double gag
And spits poor Jonah out!
Prophet's sittin' on the shore,
Lord, he's drippin' wet!

Now, I gotta' mention
. . . Gotta' mention this,
Jonah's known as awful slow
When it comes to burnin' people up.

Well, I never been to Nineveh,
Can't even spell its name,
But I been to Lo Do Denver
And, man, they got some sinners there!

So, keep your eyes wide open,
Keep them kind of large,
Jonah's headin' into town,
And the Fish ? ? ?

That slippin' Fish . . .
Is gaggin' right behind.
Well, I never been to Nineveh,
Can't even spell its name,
But I been to Lo Do Denver
And, man, they got some sinners there

I'D LIKE TO BE A DESERT RAT

I'd like to be a desert rat,
grow whiskers off my chin,
make shade when heat means "go real slow"
and wake to cooling chirps.

Orion, I'd see you face-to-face,
go fishing in the stars
that, streaming west, as silver fish
out-swim the swimming Dawn.

I'd learn how precious water is,
how spines instead of leaves
protect the core beneath the crust,
come home you cactus wrens.

Tippet dew, a sandy wash, smoke
and palo verde blue,
forgiving sin and chronic drought,
flower ocotillo.

Out here a lonely palm will stand,
but better in a grove
I'd strive to understand without,
to live the strength within.

SKIPPING STONES

When we knew what we were doing,
calm within the center,
slow and steady progress, sure and
peaceful purpose, when was

That? Caught in the undertow of
you must see ourway, we
borrow just enough history
forgetting our genius

To be dangerous. Skipping stones
across the sea just to
see how far we can throw them propels
even quicker sinking.

FRONTIER

Frontier pioneers—
fire, fear, and drought,
cycles boom and bust,
always here, always

Immediate—our need
for each other—for life
and opportunity to
abide and persevere.

YOU KNOW WHAT WATER MEANS

You know what water means

When you have to squeeze
the water from a plant
to stay alive,

You know what water means

If you're the plant
or the river
or any wild thing,

You know what water means.

O Mr. and Mrs. Minister,
do you know what water means?

O you High Court Justices,
do you know what water means?

Imagine you're a woman
storing water in an ostrich egg
for when the water disappears,

You know what water means.

Imagine you're a seed
that never knows the joy
of having roots,

You know what water means.

Imagine you're a river
or a wild thing
or a person,

You know what water means.

OUT HERE

Out here, on the high plains,
I marvel at the water trickle
a windmill flows,

All the possibilities,
all the dreams,
a hundred years or so—

To the south,
a forgotten cemetery
cows now graze

Claims a handful of
nameless homesteaders—
to the west, a ditch

That never carried
more than dreams
of irrigation bounty—
to the north, the waterless
Keota water tower—
to the east, the ruined

Grasslands of
"Government Ground"
busted into lost 160s—

New directions
brittle foundations
squeezed from the planet—

Pardon my ramblings.
In the rhythm of the rivers,
the west finds its most treasured experience.

(with Emmett Jordan)

MUSHROOM CLOUD

Mushroom cloud, smoke of Hayman fire,
rises from the notch left of Windy Peak
directly south of a Saturday evening

And billows into Sunday.
Ash rains on Denver's hypothesis.
"Stay indoors!" an urban advisory,

"Get out now!" the mountains
command. Two weeks to the day
smolders a skeleton forest,

Nothing an orange moon
hasn't mirrored before
arcs above,

Tugs to unplug our heart pumps
as she does the Sea of Cortez
for a gray whale spouting.

On the uplifted crust
of a vast and dried-up ocean,
dwelling in the heartland,

Only we
of all creatures
can imagine.

RAIN DANCE

It's easier to argue with one you love
but the argument runs the risk
of greater heat,
too much intelligence of the other
fuels the fire.

How long since each has cleared the underbrush?
They say the meadow needs a sun-cut
opening the canopy doesn't permit,
though without a sheltering enclosure the fawn
cannot test her wheels.

Always when I'm angry
I feel lavas melt,
rediscover discomposure's crack,
embarrassed— blessedly— by my ability
to throw flaming words in spurts

At everything I cultivate.
"Please forgive me"
is the only substance
of any significance
to a Rain Dance.

HAIL AND THE HOPPERS

Yellow jackets sure are greedy,
they squeeze themselves through holes
of hummingbird feeders, drown in
sugar water they intend to feed on.

Impulse, ignorance, desperation, self-
determination? Frontier pioneer
blizzard of 1886, drought of 2002,
squeezing through 'till Spring,

Will turn your stripes to the inside
if you and the neighbors can hang on,
if the rain comes, if the ice breaks,
if hail and the hoppers don't get you.

RAINDROP!

Raindrop! You lick the leaf so gently,
then you fall and kiss the ground,

How high you fell!
How welcome you decline,

The leaf bends for you
dropping out of heaven.

Why did you leave?

EPIPHANY

I had given up on the concept of rain,
I thought the steady pat-pat rattling
of drain-pipe down spouts spitting out rumble throat
tin-hearted lawn flutes a fanta-gormat,
I was wrong.

I cannot say the rain any
more than I can say my name before my
Mother first whispers a name to me, "Gregie!"
I feel a rush, a chill, I hear a howl,
I spit rain from my own chill-hearted construct,

I sense dumb porosity spilling out
every would-be every should-be.

SLOW DRIP EVENING

Drought reminds
do not haste to put away
the winter snows that
backyard fills. Decorate
with red, welcome

Them. Hang festoon
across your window sill
and spread the tree of life
across your entry way.
Call exotic birds to roost

Among your thread and
branches. Sprinkle grain
instead of salt. Fix soup.
Put out your silver birthing
spoons, invite the frosted

Moon within, read Jane
Kenyon. Let your tracks
be leavened in their traces
and your oven hold the
ozone smell of slow drip

Evening. Truckle in
down comforters, let play
bassoon and oboe, adobe
bugs in cracks and eaves.
Do not inveigh against the storm.

NOW THE DIMINISHING

Now the diminishing, the transforming.
day-old snow on the downward curve of a
spruce branch, part of you falls, part rises up.

Thump! Unassuming silent assumption:
both contribute. Your power—happenstance
and circumstance—droughts you have known

Combine to a waiting purpose, waiting for you.
No prediction can measure your cause, your
effect, no part of you is wasted, none

Wholly unexpected. A way is pared
for you. Touch the soil, join a cloud, let
go be your force, your flowing destiny.

FORGETTING

The longest day of the year
sets at 8 p.m.

In the foothills of the Colorado
mountains the year after

The very latest drought.
We had forgotten

What the trees tell
in their tightest rings

In the foothills of the Colorado
mountains. In the very

Latest drought we became
ring readers,

Now blue bells hang
from a green stem.

DOWSER

Witcher you going to believe?
The seismic engineer,
driller of holes,
guy with the nose?
Only the water knows.

A SHORT DITTY

I've got my lawn,
I've got my green,
I've got my sprinkler,

I'll turn it off,
I'll turn it brown,
I'll turn it upside down,

I guess I knew,
I guess I see,
I guess I do agree,

The human brain's
A mighty tool
But it don't make no rain.

PTERODACTYL WINGS

Grandson wants you to make pterodactyl
Wings, so he can fly through blue bright waters,
Flouncing and gurgling, his digitals
Flaying the flanks of your would be wingspan.
Imported rivers, aren't they all? Through some
Aqueduct cut from the Colorado
Or the Rhone—3 to 5 feet deep,
Cost of this enraptured precious desert
Perrier, $2. 89 per liter. We drink
And swim and watch Shrek
In this San Diego room, wondering
What American westerners can learn
Re-inventing old world ogres in their
Own image and likeness, and what's for lunch?

I'M CONFUSED

First, it's really wet. Rafting
every Spring, great fishing when
the streams subside, all the slopes
powder-full. Tourists like the place
better than any place else, Summer,
Winter, Fall, any month at all, you can
stand in the shower a really long time!

Then, the dry thing. Camping goes
poof along with the woods, got to
hand hold the hose to give the
poor median strip front door tree
just a sip, and just try to remember
which day, in what zones, at midnight
or is it before? you get to do the lawn.

Now, they say, the reservoirs are 85
percent there and so we can have an
extra watering day. Shame of it is, I
was getting used to the way it was,
you know, the scarcity thing and feeling
O.K. I can do this if we all can. So
why don't we let the reservoirs keep
the extra day? Or the farms or the fish?

FRANKLIN ST. HYBRID

I'm sharing with the neighbors this year a new form of Type-A drought-resistant dandelion. We call it the Franklin St. Hybrid. It's cultivated to duck the lowest power mower setting yet-capable of fast growing wind-blown seed stems whenever the cutting blade's not looking. Its smile is golden. Whatever the whacking, it keeps on booking; there's no awful need to rip up your gross-billed bluegrass.

Simply relax, keep your water tap turned off, uncork a cool one, and enjoy the front porch swing. It's resistant to all deplorable forms of sweat and EPA-certified pesticide, so you save-save-save on all the unfriendly expensive inputs. And the dogs love it. They'll pause frequently to salute your inviting floral display.

Now the Water Board can substitute its multi-tiered water-guzzling rate-punishment program for something that really works up a beautiful utility for nothing.

THIS YEAR'S WATER BUFFALO

This Year's Water Buffaloes Are

Two Bobs
Two Johns
Two Sandys and a Frank-Jack
Ted and Leonard
Ben
Bill and Dick
And Two Big Ralphs!

Now you know the look of the Water Buffalo

All Snort and Spit,
From the Front End Mostly Horn and Beard,
In the Middle a Gigantic Hump
To Get Over Any Way You Can,
From the Rear
A Might Heavy Load
Moving down the Road to the Water Hole.

The View at the Water Hole is delicious
To the Water Buffalo,
He Puts his Big Snout All the Way in It,
Takes a Prodigious Gulp,
Shakes his Mug 'till Flies Flee His Fur,
Makes a Grand Look Straight at his Glorious Reflection,
And Roars to Anyone Two Miles Distant

"Mighty   Pretty   Aren't   I!!"

Humble? This Guy's a Huge Bit Too Awesome for That.
He's also Gregarious,
Likes to Hang With the Herd
Until One of the Other Guys Tries to Hoof in
On His Turf.

It's then the Water Buffalo Takes to Being Part
Lawyer and Part Engineer,
Paws up a Cloud of Dust and Calls it Water.
As a Matter of Fact, Lawyers and Engineers Make
A Whole Lot More Water than Seems Possible,

The Mountains Can't Anywhere Do as Good as Half.

And Whatever an Aquifer Is
We All Know After Listening to the Water Buffalo
There's A Lot More
Or A Lot Less Water
Just Underground
Depending on
Which End of the Horn
They're Doing Battle From.

Yep,
It's a Mighty Great Country
Can Accommodate the Water Buffalo
At the Best Western
And Not Be Offended by Having to Bring
A Spare Set of Shoes to Walk Out
In!

GATHERING

YOUR SPECIAL MUSIC

When sun sets red
over the edge of reason
into the woods of faith
comes a time for cinching-up
for certain climbs ahead
mountains do not hide,
Continents wander west into them.

Gather with some friends
in ever-widening circles
where water holes begin
to ripple on a rock,
for I have seen your
special music play.

No words or signs alone
can sing the truth
that love can bring
through river canyons
when rangering.

BY THE ROADSIDE

I'm hungry, tired, miss my dog,
goofy frantic kids are throwing
rocks from bridges, tourist jeeps
drive by. I'm casting this unknown
spinner to riffles below the Riverside
Hotel, Hot Sulphur Springs. It's May,
a week before Memorial Day, these drat
wetlands are seeping through trashed-out
Hi-Tec boots, dear wife is sitting in a lawn
chair gabbing with her friends. I pop a Pop.
How a river shines, dives behind a rotting shelter log,
hisses, spits, thrusts its tongue, coils into pools,
rears to strike, then unwinds, slithers darkly
down the bank, slides to dusk, slips
to crescent moon on speckled scales,
encircles earth, reappears at dawn
with jaws agape to swallow
fisher men.

HUMID MORNING VAPOR SONG

Humid morning vapor song,
dewy grass and marshy ground,
tadpole, toad and crane, flex and swim.
Arise, fly up! You are called to worship shine,
display your feathers, skin, and beak, your metamorphic
tail, whistle, grunt, inhale, belly pull yourself to land, flashing.

TRAIL BUILDING

No Trail is the Work
Of One,
Each Length Builds
On the Length
Of Others,

Where a Trail May Lead
Is Spirit Vision
Stretched
Brow to Heel,
As
Trail

Leads on to Trail,
Where Aspen
Swim to Spruce,
Mountains
Fall Away To
the Great
Havens of the Lordly
Sky,
No Scar or Gouge
To Deluge
Ripped
How Your Turnouts
Hold
Through Contours
Of Life Zones
Habitat,
Rhythm,
Moment,
Valley,

Foothill,
Ridge and Stream
Design,
Art and

Practice,
Dwell
Within.

PEACE

Fishing is a point of view you have to want inside,
the Hope, the Fling, the Wait, the Zing, the Catch,
Peace releasing.

CANOE

Help me summon up the strength
to do the good I can each day,
at least a little space with you
between despair and opportunity

To dip my shiny stirring blade
in waters deep and welling full.
And let my muscle ache desist
to sit a-center my canoe

Quiet would you spread to me
hums and hums of sinewing,
nimble tissues at their work
of joining joy to drudgery.

Thank you for this resting me
for the whys persisting me,
I take this heel to my hand
paddle, Lord, this promised land.

AN OLD COLORADO STORY
"A MAJOR MINING ENVIRONMENTAL RESTORATION PROJECT IS AHEAD"

"As you travel along the next two miles of the San Miguel Valley, you can see the mine remediation project—pioneering new revegetation techniques and setting a national precedent for environmental remediation. The process includes precise recontouring of the tailing surface, amendment of the tailing surface with limestone and organic nutrients, and seeding with specially selected grasses and forbs to create an engineered vegetative cover."

Ouray and Telluride,
Within the mountains lie
an old Colorado story,
"There's money in those rivers,
Boys!" Vein-on-vein of twisted
silver, slag of gold is
followed muck on spoil
until the rivers bleed.
Then these wooden shanty towns,
with all their crimson-
beautied natives gone, Ute
and Southern Mountain Ute,
brilliant-bellied cutthroat
trout, bosomed ladies
laudanam-laced,
and all their sportsmen
plaintiff cry "Repay, Repay!"
so the river's purified
so mountain meadows sprout
these golfing greens,
these fly tie
shops.

I BELIEVE THERE MUST BE

I believe there must be a better place than Colorado,
I believe there must be better spruce, better peaks,
Better firmaments, I believe there must be.

I believe there must be a truer place then Colorado,
I believe there must be truer canyons, truer mesas,
Truer plains, I believe there must be.

I believe there must be a sweeter place than Colorado,
I believe there must be sweeter soils, sweeter sunsets,
Sweeter chickadees, I believe there must be.

I believe there must be a higher place than Colorado,
I believe there must be a higher sky, higher streams,
Higher lakes, I believe there must be.

I believe there must be a bluer place than Colorado,
I believe there must be a bluer place,
I believe there must be.

CLOSING UP THE CABIN

So, we clear the moth wings out we have lived with,
dog hair, spider webs, spots on kitchen, bathroom
bowls, drips beneath the sinks, blotches on the bedroom
mirror. Mice. We see ourselves, cleaning. All things we
put away, or dispose of, in their own measure have served.
Here, at this termination, we mark the season of our service
by preparing room for others.

Perfect clean like perfect service,
an aspiration, but the perfect mess we inevitably make of it
will mark the measure of our living, no matter how others
may view our housekeeping. A magpie, giant in his blackness
and the whiteness of his underbelly stands on the tip of a
young conifer, feeling he can fly when his foundation
slips. Desire lends us wings. So we clear the cabin for
the winter, hope to return when new-hatched moths are
on the wing and turning orb peeks into moth-like Spring.

RIMROCK

You stand on the edge of the rimrock,
you see the other side clearly, so close
it seems, an immense chasm between.
You have to go down, holding yourself
back every step of the way so you don't
pitch over. Then the climbing back up,
earning every inhalation. Awesome
vistas all around. Carry a couple of water
bottles! Did I say about the River? Good
sand will cradle you. The stars? Heaven
in your face as long as you can stay awake.
Someone to talk to. Or just be silent with.

THE WAY YOU'VE NOT YET BEEN

Lift your eyes to the hills,
Plant your feet among the trees,
The way that is before you
Is the way you've not yet been.
Gather in your family,
Bring along your friends,
Raise yourself for each other
Then the mountains will be seen.

AT ALL

Enjoy the time
you have today
it's very little
time at all.

Find you love
each other best
the rest will fall
away.

IN A HIGH WIND

In a high wind
plant your roots firmly
to your crown,
and bend a little.

GRACE

Pray our tongues

   Be true like streams

      Constant murmur

         Of all being.

EVAPORATION

Simple truths
water and the sun

That all is worn away
and taken up again

For blessed rain to send.

EASY ON THE WATER

Easy on the water
flip a fly
so from underneath
a graceful flight
appears

Worth a closer look,
no artifice must seem.

Slap a pool
with plated flashy spoon
and slackened line,
best to send a school
to scattering

A reel's worth of winding,
Easy on the water.

BROKEN COMPASS

How wide the mountains
and many the trails
through them,

How warm the circle
of friends around
the campfire,

How cold and lonely
to be excluded
from hearing their stories,

Freedom to express one's
values—a great and valuable
compass,

To set out exploring only
with those who share
your values—

Broken compass.

THE EAGLE OR THE OTTER

Some days you look at a river
you forget you've ever seen one,
somehow this particular river seems
so supple, loose and fine, so immediate.
You want to turn the wrong way
just to cross a bridge, you want to
climb a bluff you've always ignored.
You look over the edge, you see a path
through the reds, the goldens, round
the crook of the bend, down to the edge
of the Ripple. You feel you could peel
back your arms, stick out your chin,
lift off and skim the air and the water.
you might be the eagle or the otter.

TIMBERLINE

Ahead—who knows what?
maybe a marmot,
maybe a trout,
for sure, one of those tumble-
down snow-slide aspen
cruncher snags,

And that's just going the uphill
part. Doing down
can pound the knees
to peanut brittle
or that stiff-legged freeze-up
stuff

When you've got to throw
your hip and leg out
just to stop,
then that get-your-
butt-back-up-another
mountaintop.
So who you think left
those blazes in the trees?
And why those bear claw tracks
are higher than a man by half
and fresher than
a week ago?

Hope some dog-sized trout
are gonna' bite,
I'm fightin' off the
sit-me-down-forever
yearning kind of night,
God I hope
that's timberline in sight.

REDUX

Thanks for pointing out that "aster" derives from the Greek, meaning "starlike." On the bend of the Divide to the east and northeast of Silverton and Durango, we have looked at night straight up. They carpet the universe; at dawn they lay themselves down in the meadows bridging Stony Pass, so you can walk in glory through them—with nothing else between you and their returning after dusk—but the day's backpack to the evening's campsite.

They inhabit tidepools, too. Inspired by their luster, only humans would think of adding them to house collections. Home is where they are, not where you transport them to. The human brain's at home in the stars. Is familiar with asters and starfish where they appear in memory's treasure hall. Natural history museums and house arrays are poor reminders, fourth best to the universe, mountainside, and shore.

Disaster is the separation of beauty from life. Death always demonstrates this. Thanks for reminding me of basic derivations!

DISASTER

Disaster,
a flower separated
from its stem. Asters glorify
the universe, a mountainside.
Try to bring one home
like seastars from
the tide, the glow
that made them
so inviting for
the picking,
Gone.

YOU TRAVEL LIGHT

You travel light.
You carry a singing fish
wrapped in meandering ribbons,
you have deliveries to make.
But you do not hurry, you
enjoy murmuring to the fish.

ANY GOOD CAMP STOVE

Ice is tropical steam
stored up in glaciers
left over from love.
You can auger a drill

Hole through its column
of climate changes.
Any good camp stove
can fill your cup again.

THE HILLS ARE ALWAYS THERE

The hills are always there.
We can dig at them, spread our
gathering and manufacturing edifices
across their graces, remove
and contour them. Beneath,
they will always slip slowly away,
while the earth pushes them back
up. If we luck, we can absorb their
momentum, in the way we pitch
our inclination towards their tilt.

WONDERING

Sand time, water time, rock time,
star time, waves to the shore,
shadows on ripples. We cast
our lengths only because the
sun would have it so, standing
on the edge on sand on water
on rocks on stars,
Wondering.

MANY FEATHERS AND SOME GLUE

If I simply could, I would catch for you
a current, many feathers, and some glue,
we'd go perch upon a crag and watch for
sailing weather, the kind that binds the glue.
You could launch and eddy up, I would
spiral after you, we'd both be tiny
soaring dots upon the billow cloud aloft,
we could see how rain is made. And, befall,
should we grow enough of being blue
and simply drop away and softly land.

HYDRAULIC PRINCIPLE

The body's a canteen
for the soul.

BLACK SONGBIRD SUNFLOWERS

You can't start over, you can only start
again, over and over. Rain and snow
fall when vapor climbs in air when all is
full again, dropping possibilities.
Always a tell, a wind you remember
comes in, a red-headed bird stirs round
the interval between thaw and freezing.
You hear the flickers go rat-a-tatter, rat-a-
tatter. Listen. You can hear the beat of
wings of earthworms surfacing, ground pawing
horses throw their magnificent nostrils
open. You stand to borrow longer days
you thought you'd forgotten. Put out seeds,
black songbird sunflowers, gathering bowls.

AQUIFERS

Laws of nature, laws of human nature,
a law for nature and for humans springing
from where the river and the aquifers
interconnect at the place where waters
meet a daily need with universal appeal.

The waters serve, we with them, a public
need for a public good. Relax, reflect,
revitalize, rejoice, work, work, work,
Blessings are of water and the spirit,
good company, opportunity to commit

And recommit to community. In this
our Western place, from deep within
subterranean sources, springs
feed the rivers, feed us, feed
all fellow living manifestations.

WOODSPEOPLE

Throw out the map,
those who came and went
drew it—as they knew it
we may say, faithfully—
only so far as they
could see to it.
Who follows must
conceive a contour
different, because the land
adds and subtracts
from itself in order
to confuse confidences.

Woodspeople trust most
in fresh experiences,
scat, bent
grasses,
hoof
prints.

SOME DAY

We shall forget the key
And walk to where—
                    Walk to where—
                    Wherever may be,

And forget to door
The lock—
                    And free some other visitor—
                    To enjoy,

And turn the river
Back to itself—
                    And the star to where—
                    May wherever be.

MARES' TAILS

When the sky is full and high
of mares' tails, I would like to ride
on nothing but the air
and silver bridle slip me,

For when a pillow kingdom's come
golden arcs declining,
wild ponies range the other side
galloping, galloping.

WELCOME!

Welcome to Colorado,
welcome home!—
hope you feel good
about moving on—
moving here,

Where'd you come from—
Kansas, Ohio, California,
Bosnia, Pakistan,
Israel?— welcome home,
welcome here! A basic

Truth, beside the land,
beside the sky—all of us,
we entered here, Ute,
Cheyenne—moving up
the rivers, moving 'cross

The plains, from Santa Fe,
Spain, Africa, China, Japan,
Ireland—on horse, on foot,
board the Iron Horse, board
the aeroplane—our oldest

Ruins—why, just yesterday—
people into Hovenweep
settling the Southwest sun,
moving disappearing water
from disappearing creeks,

They built towers, too—
looking for enemies? Looking
for friends moving up the trade
routes from Central, from South
America—like we they pray,

Make mistakes, cruel and kind—
families, discover much, prosper,
bust out—love the whirling storms
just as suddenly, sky-on-fire scarlet,
swoop of hawk, sweep of the long 360,

Lope of coyote, ponderosa pollen—
miller moths moving on through,
fluttering round the lights—
borrowing the land, the sky,
hatch on the waters, borrowing on.

HEAR THE WATERS SORT THEMSELVES

Chuck Lile, Dear Friend,
we'll miss you when the waters sing
in the Weminuche and skies are brilliant blue
or scarlet, when lightning slashes and thunder rolls
from the Window to the Pyramid. We'll miss you
when elk bugle and aspen burn with gold,
when our horses strain on the uphill march and sizzle
of the frying-pan holds our dinner. We'll look for you
when our stories lengthen into evening and hear
the waters sort themselves between
San Juan and Rio Grande.

FODDER FOR A FUTURE WORK

Planting dryland winter wheat
in the high plains rides a chance of rain,
farmer's rite of scarcity and necessity,
an even-money bet with mother nature.
Bet against hail disease pests mis-timed moisture,
will the seeds germinate go dormant re-energize?
Will they become flour and bread,
ride the winter storms into cycle of Spring
and Summer harvest?
Yes, my dear wife, my dear children,
you will! For I have loved and cared enough
to believe in you and the continuing
of all we have planted.

(with Emmett Jordan for Bill Kuntz)

CINCH MY FILAMENT

OLD PANTHERS

Old panthers, latch them to a swivel,
let them fly. No need to hook a fish,
just being on the water's fine--
in every pool, a face I've loved
is looking back. Linger for
a moment, then is gone
to ripples....

BEING WINGS

Find our Lord
In the tramp of earth,
Find our Lord
In the sleep of snow,
Find our Lord
In the mountain cirques,
Find our Lord
In the sounding keeps.

Open air running brook
Tramp of earth sleep of snow
Mountain cirques sounding keeps
Wringing winds being wings.

BROOKE

Good fishes to you!

May they glide to your fancy,
may you watch over them,
may the waters catch you up,
Bless and heal you,

May your spine always be
the Great Divide,
may you return love

To all love belongs.

BLESSINGS ON YOUR WAY

Blessings on your way,
may the soil bear you up,
may the horizon always stretch before you

And the stars flicker with fun.
May all you learn and all you teach,
and all you learn by teaching,

Always lead you on
as long as mountains sing
the mountain waters.

And when they join the sea again
and beyond, may you know the peace
that passes understanding.

CEDAR

The finest my father could do
was take to the woods
to go fishing

My brothers and me

Could see him big grinning
the closer we'd get to the water
he in the middle

Between us and the pour

Of those hours together
cedar to follow to get back
to the river.

GENTLE NIGHT

Gentle night, go softly out,
go softly out this land,
gently lead the light away
and every creature . . .
fold, and every flower
fold,

Tuck away the marsh,
the thrush, tuck away the
water jar,
Smooth the rub, the catch,
the stretch

That will not fit, the raw
of maiming words,
the hurt that will not heal,

Settle on the lids,
the lips, the finger tips.

THE MOTHER LOAD

This is the promised season of gold
the lookers came looking for,

Golden folding aspen leaves,
when you go looking for them

This is the season of the big return,
the silver season

Brooks and fishes flip,
in the lowest ebb of pick

When you go looking for
the Mother Load.

BUCKETS TO THE MOON

Buckets to the moon
you and I can only know the tunes
we've carried here and there,

tunes I've whispered in your ear,
you to me, us to us,
stringing little water pockets,

tunes in little water buckets,
stringing little water pockets
to the moon.

ROCK CREEK

Good to see you mountains,
good to hear you streams.
I've been a long time comin',
you called me in my dreams.
Who says we need the city
and the dyin' midst the din?
When we're up on Rock Creek
we learn to live again.

FRESHET YOUNG AM I

Freshet young am I
barely know my strength
in jagged peaks arise
of ice and wilderness

Seized of summer short
asleep in berry bogs
I wake to sudden drops
the width of roaring rain

I take the days that granted
slip away with me
over jamming logs I dance
high and clear and plain

At the touch of every shore
hope and sorrow, joy and pain
always run another chance
to whirl, ripple, plunge and bend

And when it's delta time again
when I'm laid a mile flat
I think about the course I've run
freshet young I am.

WEDGES

How do geese choose who goes first
flying wedges across the full moon?
Your turn today, Joan, give a honk
when you want to rise up, we'll
be along! One moment a graceless
throng, the next, wingtips stretched,
each one crying out to the other.
We're on our way, Grace! Then
leaving your feet to follow George
and Pete. You flap away, head
to the invisible, right behind the
guy in front of you >>>>>

MAY FOR YOU

May for you deep, deep blue of the sky not
fall down for you but far, far within the
farthest stars for you, may they shine for you,
may the stars of the sky always shine within for you,

And for you may the waters of the earth not
swell sound within for you but clear, clear within
their banks for you, may the waters of the earth
swell within their banks for you, so clear within for you,

And may for you each of the days of the world not
so ever rise within for you but here, here so ever rise
within for you, may they always rise within for you,
may the days of the world always rise within for you.

WHEN I AM WITH YOU

Deep strength comes coursing through,
swells with wanderlust
into green and blue,
climbs on crimson clouds,
leaps a moon that's shining full.

When I am with you
birds of paradise fly for peaks,
whales with wings of sirens
skim the sea for ship-wrecked sailors
chorusing.

When I am with you
cinnamons paw the sky for honey,
herons wade in firefalls
to spear the streaking fishes
of the sun.

WHEN THE MAYOR DOMO CALLS

When the Mayor Domo calls
to apple bee and blossom
I'll be sleeping underneath

The sweetest song a meadow
lark can sing,

And take my shovel up the
elbow of the ditch to hack
the stubborn elm's

Forestalling grip.

COME ON BACK ALL YOU GRACES

Come on back all you graces,
Come on back to me now,
Come on back all you graces,
Come on back to me now.

Courage, patience, humor,
Plain speaking tolerance,
Grit, passion, wit to believe
My own special insignificance.

Come on back all you graces,
Come on back to me now,
Come on back all you graces,
Come on back to me now.

Those I've looked up to,
Those who said go to it,
Those who let go greatly when
They just knew it was time to.

Come on back all you graces,
Come on back to me now,
Come on back all you graces,
Come on back to me now.

Yes, you can. Yes, you will.
I'm so glad I could help.
Yes I believe you've got to
See, in your own way, through.

Come on back all you graces,
Come on back to me now,
Come on back all you graces,
Come on back to me now.

POOL

What about a pool
attracts? Peace of it,
danger of falling in,
bugs?

A pool looks back,
you see your self
within, above,
behind....

You desire rocks to throw
you think you see a fish,
cloud fleet passes
over you, you

      disappear.

FISHERMAN'S KNOT

Lord, my hands tremble,
I must take off my glasses,
hold the line to my eye
and twist three or four
times. This space between
the loop, Lord, help me
hold it here, grant me
just a little more light
to thread the gap between
my thumb and forefinger,
let me cinch my filament
to your swivel. Lord, I am
complete, I hear the stream
behind me continuing.

LATE ARRIVAL

Perfect beam of light from a far blue hill

       slants a
            long
                  bright
                       path

through the open threshold, and lands
            at the base of the pressure tank.

I flip the pump handle on,
stop cock flat against the uplift pipe.

                    Subterranean
                    thrust up-rushes
                    to water heater,
                    tap, sink, shower,
                    bowl that cleans
                    away what I have
                    drawn my strength
from.

Across Elk Creek draw,

              seven
              layer hills
              blue
              on
              blue
              build,
              recede.

Now, dusk, now!

I DRAW FROM SUCH A LITTLE WELL

I draw from such a little well,
I tap a fractured aquifer,
I draw from such a little well
in gallons quite unnoticeable.

The woman at the well,
she hands a cup to me,
I draw from such a little well
I tap when I am able.

The man he comes to me,
he calls me by my name,
stands the gauging rod before
me and sees that I am filled.

The woman at the well,
she hands a cup to me,
I draw from such a little well
I tap when I am able.

I'll never be the river,
I'll never be the lake,
I'll never be the ocean,
then, her cup, I take with me.

The woman at the well,
she hands a cup to me,
I draw from such a little well
I tap when I am able.

WILLIAM STAFFORD'S YARN

William Stafford at his desk in early morning took his pen in hand and
let the pen tell him where it wanted to go. Most often the pen stayed
within the room and played, as a cat will, with a ball of yarn. The yarn
unraveled itself, going where it wanted to go. Many mornings the yarn
took itself out the door, down the street, down to the river, beyond the
lights, over the hill, and the one after that, to a place where the yarn
would un-ball itself on the shore of the river of stars.
Each morning the yarn would pick one of the morning stars to visit.
Sky, Open Doors, The Sleep of Blue, Clear Days, Promises, Father,
Mother, Others, The Blue Voice, Roof All Day, Arches, Turn Away,
Reach Far Within Me, So Sure, Whatever Is Hiding, Nothing. Then the
yarn would roll itself through the window back up to have coffee with
William Stafford, his cat, and his pen about the time dawn began to
look through for them.

DROPLET

Sometimes I'm a pouter
Sometimes a spouter
Sometimes I'm pouring
Precious liquid

Fresh from silver pewter.
Sometimes I'm the spark
Sometimes the wick
Sometimes I'm a candle tall

Shining from a silver candlestick.
Sometimes I'm a telescope
Sometimes the microscope
Sometimes I see the universe

Ablaze a precious droplet.

SAM AND JACQUELINE, JACQUELINE AND SAM

Sam and Jacqueline, Jacqueline and Sam,
to her he was always returning—
she would send him out by day
to gather the news,

In gathering the news, he was always thinking—
aw! Here's something interesting
Jacqueline would like to hear—she his
compass, he her map.

There were so many places she could never go
she didn't need—content with his going
on the promise of his many, very many,
returnings—he for her, she for him,

In this, their love would fill every distance—
capitols, important people, many good deeds,
the great ideas, yes, but Aw! her grace!
Home to Sam—dear Jacqueline—

Kind and loving Jacqueline, devoted Sam.
Such a gift as partners may bring to each other,
children, grandchildren, their joy, their fears—
in the house on the hill, where the sun

Above the Florida fills a breakfast nook,
arcs over the land of the Utes, sets to the West
of the La Platas—hill-on-hill to reach such
a sky as river blessings drop such

A great and holy love from—Sam and Jacqueline.

SAM AND LEONARD

"Hey Sammy, I'm Over Here You Little Sonavabitch!"
Helene Monberg yelled across a crowded Washington, D.C.
Restaurant.

Bob Barkley, Manager of the Northern Colorado Water
Conservancy District, liked telling this story. Helene wrote a
cobbled-together inside-the-capitol water report; scooped
the rest of the media regularly about Western water projects—
she'd interlineate practically every sentence with a word or two
practically everyone else had left out. Helene was rough and
fresh and full of textual content

Like bolo-tied San Maynes of Durango, Colorado, and that
Southern Ute, the square-rigged Leonard Burch, who constantly
accompanied him on these "When-Do-We-Indians-Finally-Get-
Our-Water-Back" breakfast trips to the gut of Government.

Carl Hayden and the Udall Boys were busy going about the
Central Arizona Project—this the way Helene saw it—
while Sam and Leonard kept on breaking their eggs
in pursuit of justice

Until the big clout of the Lower Basin States in 1968 yelled
"Ouch" to the tribes whose ancestral home nestled high up
the Great Bend of the Continental Divide.

And that was just the start. Those who cut the gold and silver
from that Native land had lodged a legacy of acid-spoil piles
draining into the Animas. Water politics had its toxic, too.
"Let the River be a river!" wrung its cry of truth from natural
advocates, but all that other development left the Utes—
Southern and Ute Mountain, who had the earlier claims—bereft.

Three decades more—Sam and Leonard knock-knock-knocking
on the door—and the San Juan's greatest treasure, to drink
and grow these Tribes from mountain streams, will it seems
be a returning measure of Western civilization.

Sam and Leonard, steady and durable friends, turned their spades
to water, and now have passed—Sam just yesterday. Colorado
and the Country? Richer for them.

AGUA FUEGO

"You are a lake."
So you paint me blue or gray
ruffled lines moving towards you
or—contrary—push away urgently.
Perhaps you catch a barque

At the moment your hair-tip brush pens
a spear point to the prow of a trailing wake.
Perhaps you hear the rotor's unsteady hum
suggest a buckling fisherman, you
prick a scratch of light for beacon

You'll never get him to.
If you are writing this, dusk propels
your protean hand towards an ending,
in 15 minutes a chill will stymie
your force

And I remain looking up from my Vulcan-
vulva depths hallowed by collapse of three-
fold mountain fires. As you pass, I shall
wick another flame, for you, for all you
conjured up, for all you have absorbed of me.

ODE TO THE WATER COMMISSIONERS

Voices of the Natural Stream

O you Commissioners
O you dividers of me

O you who deliver me
plum peach cherry grape

Cow fox egret sheep
rapid kayak turbine reach

Fire plug O garlic sprout
black diamond run

The greenback trout
O sudsy mug

My river call
my head gate wheel

My tumble weir
O falling wild

Delivery room
my civilizing scarcity.

THE TIGER AND THE CHALICE

There's a tiger on their lifeboat,
a chalice for their lips,
readers at their stations
discuss great mysteries,

How the peoples may survive
by learning not to trust
monger-roaring advocates
of jugular politics,

How men and women serve
by being solar stills,
leaching out the salt
to fill a water cup,

How men and women carry
a code that's hardly secret,
hand the cup of water out
is written plain and simple.

PEACH TULIP

One stem,
One leaf,

Earth air
Water fire

Beyond
Being
Beautiful,

Stellar
You.

MERCATOR PROJECTIONS

Mercator projections bring you here, exactly.
How to show a globe when all that goes before
goes flat? Place yourself at either pole
and look back, possibilities at both opposites
appear bigger than they are extreme
and the center elongates around a band
that plays upon the shores of oceans barely
heard, though thundering at your feet.

Magellan took a spear in the throat proving his
command to native disputants, this Portuguese
expert sailing for Spain—trusted by neither—
scourge of his own crew, set the course of future
Explorer Kings and Presidents, their spine-
compasses riveted to the same curvature.
Footprints left in the sand—by Friday—
what visitors can leave and best return to.

MAY 1

drips snow drops
to cherry tree feet,
back fence gives back
little whitecaps
night floated down

to cap the wooden peaks
nailed in a row praying
morning steam,

I see Saturday proclaim
cleansing of the leaves
and leave

my many snow shovels be.

MOUNTAINS ARE MY CHURCH

I often hear a Coloradan say
mountains are my Church;

In May the Goldenpea appears
in spaces Ponderosa canopy;

June your Potentilla, used for treating
burns and expediting childbirth,

Higher up the Buttercups, at timberline
where Columbine; July, as shadows

Of the early evening slant across a
mountain meadow, filament Primrose

Opens yellow pollen to the pink night
moth, edible roots, cure for coughs,

Colds, asthmatic troubles soothe;
orange sneezeweed for August,

Navajo remedy for vomiting, salve
for pains in chest and shoulders;

Violet monkshood for September,
powerful helmet-shaped heart

Stimulant, the European variety
virulently poisonous; then the snows

That say goodbye to blossoms
begin to dress the watershed

For April's blessing yet to come.

DIFFERENT TUNE

I'd like to empty my jar
of every anthem I know
and carry that jar
thirsting for a tune
as far as I may

No water I carry
when my jar is full
or when I pour it out
if it does not sing
but rains only fire

I would fill my jar
hearing of distant waters
healing a cup at a time
held in every hand
of every person singing

A different tune.

THEY HAVE MADE OF SAM FRODO SPIDERMAN

They have made of Sam Frodo Spiderman
magnificent flickering imprint images
of heroes who carried me

Up the mountain, through the city—
tall lonely young adult dorm library seminary—
into the fathering of my years.

And I am wed to the smart blond beauty
I feared I would never meet, and our hairs
are growing silver

In the gurg of the children of our children's
chortles. I can hear them shrieking
hosannas for the seeing of their cousins

Pull to the curb in the white Subaru
and spill out—I went fishing for these golden trout
the day after the day we started out.

There is no other way but the way to the Pass,
and I am so much nearer now—and you beside me
crick in your hip, our Kelty Packs strapped

To the forward pull, you for now you for now
you for now beside me.

SPARROWS

Laugh the night and listen,
on the mountain clear we
to sparrows pass

And fly away,
fly way and share
all we share and never can

Secure. Laugh the night
and listen off and on
our way,

Can you hear me now?
On the mountain clear we
to sparrows pass

And fly away. Fly way
and share all we never
can secure.

Essay

JOHN WESLEY POWELL, SCIENTIST, POET, AND BOTCHED POLITICIAN:
How a Non-College Graduate Invented from the Rhythms of Nature a Western Persona

~

The Colorado Plateau, A Book of Revelations

Explorer, writer, teacher, scientist, public speaker, government official, and son of a Methodist minister, John Wesley Powell saw the West—particularly the canyons of the Colorado Plateau—as a "Book of Revelations in the rock-leaved Bible of geology." [1]

Director of the U.S. Geological Survey and Bureau of Ethnography after twice running the Colorado River, he was an insatiable student of the West's aridity and Native peoples.[2] He believed that cooperative use of the land and water would be essential to everyone's success.

Opposing corporate monopolies with a passion, Powell held that Government should employ unbiased judgment—aided by a careful study of Nature—to help citizens accommodate themselves to living in community in a severe and majestic water-scare land.

Quite simply Powell loved the West. I see him as a paradigm Westerner. He believed in humanity's basic goodness and honesty, and service to others as the clearest marker of civilization: "All love of industry, all love of integrity, all love of kindred, all love of neighbor, all love of country, and all love of humanity is expressed in labor for others."[3]

Development interests and Western boomer politicians thought him a crackpot menace. He's alive with us today because we are living his experience.

What is that experience?

Awe, Ah, Yes!—Diligent Inquiry and Observation yielding Profound Wonder at what has come before that surrounds us. The passion of the Western mind is to hypothesize, to test the hypothesis, to see if it works, to relate cause and effect, to teach, explain, and learn, to witness the design of the Universe—found within everyone and everything in the minutest of particles to the immensity of way-upon-way orbit-on-orbit moving elliptically—to paint, to sing, to dance, to agree and disagree, and yet to arrive back again at the interrelationship community portends. A fundamental discovery is that every particle of matter in the universe attracts every other particle with a force proportional to the product of their masses and inversely proportional to the square of the distance between them (courtesy Newton).[4]

Perhaps, Powell's most notable trait was his ability to invent himself as he went along. He did not have a college degree when he began teaching at Illinois Wesleyan.[5] He convinced the State Normal University of Illinois to help him go on specimen collection summer field seasons to Colorado in 1867 and 1868. At Hot Sulphur Springs in 1868, talking with a mountain man, Jack Sumner, who then accompanied him, Powell conceived the 1869 Colorado River run.

Through that voyage and its sequel, Scientist-Adventurer-Philosopher-Poet, Powell gave voice to the inspiring force of rock, water, and erosion in creating that most magnificent of all chasms, the Grand Canyon. While the scientific method might be seen as requiring explanations of the universe that are concretely predictive, and therefore impersonal, mechanistic, and structural,[6] Powell did not speak or act as if explanations of the universe must be systematically cleansed of all spiritual and human qualities.

Powell's chief interests were structural geology, a branch of science he and his men virtually invented, and the overall relation of people to the arid lands of the West.[7] He hypothesized and documented that erosion—not sudden cataclysm—was the architect of the vast canyon land system. His persistent questioning and explanation led to a model for erosion applicable the world over.[8] Historian William Goetzmann describes him as "a scientist of brilliant lucidity with the imagination of a conjurer."[9]

Rhythmic Cadence, Symbolic Allusion, and Science

So let us go now to the River with Powell and see how—Geologist and Rhetorician—through rhythmic cadence and symbolic allusion, with its source in the Bible and—terrifically—in the land itself, he unfolds to the Nation the glory he beholds.

> We have looked back unnumbered centuries into the past, and seen the time when the schists in the depths of the Grand Canyon were first formed as sedimentary beds beneath the sea; we have seen this long period followed by another of dry land—so long that every hundreds or perhaps thousands of feet of beds were washed away by the rains; and, in turn, followed by another period of

ocean triumph, so long that at least ten thousand feet of sandstones were accumulated as sediments, when the sea yielded dominion to the powers of the air, and the region was again dry land. But aerial forces carried away the ten thousand feet of rocks, by a process slow yet unrelenting, until the sea again rolled over the land, and more than ten thousand feet of rocky beds were built over the bottom of the sea; and then again the restless sea returned, and the golden purple and black hosts of heaven made missiles of their own misty bodies—balls of hail, flakes of snow, and drops of rain—and when the storm of war came, the new rocks fled to the sea. Now we have canyon gorges and deeply eroded valleys, and still the hills are disappearing, the mountains themselves are wasting away, the plateaus are dissolving, and the geologist in the light of the past history of the earth, makes prophecy of a time when this desolate land of Titanic rocks shall become a valley of many valleys, and yet again the sea will invade the land, and the coral animals build their reefs in the infinitesimal laboratories of life, and lowly beings shall weave nacre-lined shrouds for themselves, and the shrouds shall remain entombed in the bottom of the sea, when the people shall be changed, by the chemistry of life, into new forms; monsters of the deep shall live and die, and their bones be buried in the coral sands. Then other mountains and other hills shall be made into beds of rock, for a new land, where new rivers shall flow.

Thus ever the land and sea are changing: old lands are buried, and new lands are born, and with advancing periods new complexities of rock are found; new complexities of life are evolved.[10]

Today, by raft, we can set forth on the River and see exactly how Nature's detail evokes exaltation.

The Geologist As Poet

Vying with surveyor Ferdinand Hayden for the services of the artist Thomas Moran—who had painted *The Grand Canyon of the Yellowstone* as a member of a Hayden expedition into Wyoming—Powell led Moran into the visitation that produced *The Chasm of the Colorado*. Powell insisted that the canyon could not be truly apprehended until one had descended into its depths. Although from the rim with the river snaking far away and thin in the midst of a vast canvas, Moran's panorama does invoke the gut of a primordial landscape pregnant with potential for new birth.

I love Joni Louise Kinsey's treatment of how Powell influenced the heart of this incredible painting.

> The question of redemption, finally, is at the center of *The Chasm of the Colorado*, literally and figuratively. Powell's terms for the action of water in the desert were not accidental; it could either "degrade" or "redeem," according to divine or human intervention. It could erode the land, in flash floods or in a gradual wearing of the soil, evaporate so dramatically as to wither everything, or come in sufficient amounts as to allow for the creation of a variety of forms of life. The land was one of extremes, physically and socially, with the great disparity of fortunes to be made or lost. In Moran's image the duality is there as threatening—the storm and the winding river—and as creative, when these two acts of water create new life and new forms.[11]

I have not seen Powell described as being a poet. As I see him, I name him so. The way he describes what he admires most is full of poetical expression. In writing of evolution, he points to language as the epitome of "human selection" invoking the human nightingale poet whose song endures.

> By human endeavor man has created speech by which he may express his thought. The nightingale sings to his mate; the poet sings to mankind. The song of the

nightingale dies with the passing of the zephyr; the song of the poet lives for ages.[12]

And here is Powell, music of the rivers singing:

The rainbow is not more replete with hues. But form and color do not exhaust all the divine qualities of the Grand Canyon. It is the land of music. The river thunders in perpetual roar, swelling in floods of music when the storm gods play upon the rocks and fading away in soft and low murmurs when the infinite blue of heaven is unveiled. With the melody of the great tide rising and falling, swelling and vanishing forever, other melodies are heard in the gorges of the lateral canyons, while the waters plunge in the rapids among the rocks or leap in great cataracts. Thus the Grand Canyon is a land of song. Mountains of music swell in the rivers, hills of music billow in the creeks, and meadows of music murmur in the rills that ripple over the rocks. Altogether it is a symphony of multitudinous melodies. All this is the music of waters. The adamant foundations of the earth have been wrought into a sublime harp, upon which the clouds of the heavens play with mighty tempests or with gentle showers.[13]

For such passages, I consider Powell to be a practicing master of that form of poetry we know as the prose poem.

When he wrote of the rangelands and forests that today make up most of the public lands in the intermountain West, he turned directly to poetry in metaphor of the hydrological cycle.

Sun is the father of Cloud.
Cloud is the mother of Rain.
Sun is the ruler of Wind.
Wind is the ruler of Rain.
Fire is the enemy of Forest.

Water is the enemy of Fire.
Wind feeds Forest, and Rain gives it drink.
Wind joins with Fire to destroy Forest.
Constant Rain battles with fickle Wind
And mad Fire to protect Forest.
So Climate decks the land with Forest.[14]

His Fascination With Native Americans

In his survey of the Colorado Plateau, Powell encountered Native Americans. Fascinated with them, he understood to study their ways and became director of the Bureau of Ethnology, the first effort of the United States Government to record and preserve the Nation's rich anthropological heritage. With colleagues he commissioned and trusted, he pursued these studies and issued numerous reports at the same time he was directing the U.S. Geologic Survey, the first scientific agency dedicated to the study of the country's land and water.

Here at the intersection of Native Americans, land and water, and a nation of new settlers, Powell makes many of his best contributions to our historical, scientific, and contemporary experience. On the ground experience came before his many years at a Washington, D.C. desk.

In 1870, Powell traveled with Mormon missionary Jacob Hamblin across the Colorado Plateau from Kanab to the Hopi mesas. He learned close up how Mormon and Native Americans in this part of the arid country operated community water systems.[15] These communities sharply contrasted from the Shivwits and Southern Paiutes who lived a harsh existence, depending on the harvest of wild fruits, native grains, yucca, small game, and grasshoppers.[16]

The Mormon communities spread themselves by sending out missionaries whose job it was select a town site that would be the center of neighboring farms. Working under a bishop, the new arrivals would fence the farms and "make the canals and minor water-ways necessary to the irrigation of the land. The water-ditch and fence of the farm are common property."[17] Mormon irrigation had commenced in Utah in 1847.[18] By 1865, there were 277 canals in Utah, with an average length of 3.7 miles each, the farms being relatively close to the water source. In comparison the first two 1870 Colorado Union Colony canals were 16 and 36 miles long.[19]

A Navajo boy guided Powell and Hamblin onto the Hopi mesa at Oraibi. Here is Powell's description of the Oraibi gardens:

> After dinner, we descended from the table-land on which we had been riding, into a deep valley, and having crossed this, commenced to ascend a steep rocky mesa slope by a well-worn trail, and were surprised, on approaching the summit, to find the slope terraced by rude masonry, which had evidently been made with great labor. Theses terraces, two or three acres in all, were laid out in nice little gardens, carefully irrigated by training water from a great spring in little channels along the garden plats. Here we found a number of men, women and children from the town of Oraibi gathering their vegetables. They received us with a hearty welcome and feasted us on melons.[20]

Powell visited seven Hopi "towns," as he called them, staying a total of two months studying their language, customs, and religion. He described the careful way they grew corn of different colors and made a marvelous sheet of paper-like bread we recognize as tortillas. He also described kiva ceremonies he was privileged to witness.

Powell himself became fluent in most of the region's native tongues. He and his colleagues compiled 200 vocabularies, and in 1877, he published one of his most significant works, the *Introduction to the Study of Indian Languages.*[21] In keeping with his belief in the value of irrigated agriculture, he thought the Indian reservations should be irrigated, and expert farmers sent to help them.[22]

His Water And Land Use Vision

In his 1879 *Arid Lands Report to Congress,*[23] Powell identified principles of climate, necessity, law, and use remarkably similar to those the Colorado Territorial Supreme Court had announced in its 1872 *Yunker v. Nichols*[24] opinion and the prior appropriation provision of the State's 1876 Constitution:[25]

The ancient principles of common law applying to the use of natural streams, so wise and equitable in a humid region, would, if applied to the Arid Region, practically prohibit the growth of its most important industries.

. . . .

If there be any doubt of the ultimate legality of the practices of the people in the arid country relating to water and land rights, all such doubts should be speedily quieted through the enactment of appropriate laws by the national legislature. Perhaps an amplification by the courts of what has been designated as the natural right to the use of water may be made to cover the practices now obtaining; but it hardly seems wise to imperil interests so great by intrusting them to the possibility of some future court made law.[26]

Powell emphasized that priority of utilization, based on seniority of rights, should apply in times of short supply based on the "necessities of the country."[27] He would limit the water anyone could appropriate to water actually used; his caveat was that water ought to be tied to the land permanently, a position he reasserted when serving as a member of the Public Lands Commission.[28]

Like the Native Americans who animated his ethnology work,[29] Powell saw the hand of the Great Spirit in the blessing and the working of water. "It may be anticipated that all the lands redeemed by irrigation in the Arid Region will be highly cultivated and abundantly productive, and agriculture will be but slightly subject to the vicissitudes of scant and excessive rainfall."[30] Climate, flood and drought, the power of divinely-inspired human labor teamed with natural cosmic forces to make a settling place through science, engineering, law, individual and community enterprise, and enlightened public policy—Powell harnessed Stephen Long's desert view and William Gilpin's garden view[31] into a vision of government in service to the cause of Western settlement.

Powell saw the necessity of invoking the power of the national government to aid the farmer; otherwise, corporate monopolies not animated by the public interest would control the scarce water resource.

His vision started with cooperative efforts, like those of the Mormons in Utah and the Union Colony in Colorado, to construct ditches from the streams to the land.[32] Inevitably, however, the settlers could not—within the limits of their own labor and finances—construct the reservoirs that would be needed to compensate for nature's yearly watershed rhythm of a flood of water off the mountains from spring snowmelt, then a drought when the heat of mid-summer requires crop water but the streams ebb low.[33]

Powell advocated the organization of irrigation and land use districts, and supported laws that would institutionalize the ability of Western settlers to survive and enjoy living on the land.[34]

> A series of alternate droughts and flash floods during the late 1880's and early 1890's brought [Western farmers to] the belated realization that they could not maintain their farms unless they stabilized their water supplies by building larger reservoirs and stronger dams and canals than those they had attained so far through private effort.[35]

With congressional funding, the U.S. Geological Survey produced a survey of potential reservoir sites and a short-lived piece of Powell-proposed legislation to withdraw reservoir sites from settlement under the Homestead laws,[36] so they would be available for use as needed in the future.[37]

Powell envisioned segmenting major rivers into a series of "natural districts" or "hydrographic basins" for the resolution of land and water problems; each district would own the water within its boundaries, and each landowner in the district would share in the water and water decision making.[38]

Botched Politician

From being on the ground, Powell realized that the standard survey grid and the 160-acre Homestead Act tract plunked down on mountain or plains terrain in the dry country made no sense. He advocated 2560-acre pasturage farms and 80-acre irrigation tracts; he wanted the Geological Survey to parcel out tracts based on a sensible view of the available resource. For grazing he advocated community common range as the Spanish villages in New Mexico had practiced since the 17th century; for water sharing he also favored a community approach.[39] Representative Patterson of Colorado called Powell a "charlatan in science and intermeddler in affairs of which he has no proper conception."[40]

When "Big Bill Stewart" of Nevada returned to the Senate in 1887 on a platform of free silver and irrigation, he thought Powell to be an irrigation advocate. Of course Powell was more than that, he believed in sensible land use, taking into account the limited nature of the West's resources, particularly its water.

In 1888 Representative George Symes of Colorado, sensitive to the anger of his constituents against land speculators, inserted an amendment that withdrew from settlement "all lands made susceptible of irrigation" by the reservoirs and canals which the Geologic Survey would locate. This withdrawal would aid better development and water use, but its effect was to suspend all existing land laws for the irrigable lands.[41] At first Stewart went along, but when it became clear Powell would release no lands for irrigation until the entire reservoir and canal survey was complete, Stewart exploded and successfully got the reservoir survey extinguished.

Powell was not cowed; addressing the Irrigation Congress in the early 1890s he warned there was not enough water to irrigate all the lands the dreamers had in mind, and the dreamers would reap a harvest of litigation.

> I tell you, gentlemen, you are piling up
> a heritage of conflict and litigation
> over water rights, for there is not
> sufficient water to supply these lands.[42]

Nevertheless, his vision of local water districts in charge of water rights and decision making—aided by national legislative and administrative policy—has been followed throughout the West, at least in part, through local district sponsorship and operation of reclamation projects.

Like Jefferson before him, he foresaw the West's future in terms of an enduring agrarian democracy; instead we are the great urbanizing democracy, now looking to our agricultural base not only for the food it grows but the water itself to nurture urban growth.

Paradigm Westerner

In Powell we see the paradigm Western persona: optimistic and realistic, student and risk-taker, community-minded independent, and most of all, a lover of this magnificent country dedicated to its future.

When we run the River, we shall hear his voice.

Footnotes

[1] Joni Louise Kinsey, Thomas Moran and the Surveying of the American West 111 (1992).

[2] Starting with his on-the-ground research, Powell spent much of his professional life teaching about the experience of Native Americans, Hispanos, and European/American immigrant communities in settling the arid lands of the Americas. See Justice Gregory J. Hobbs, Jr., "The Role Of Climate In Shaping Western Water Institutions," 7 Univ. Denv. Water Law Review 1-46 (2003).

[3] Quoted in William deBuys, Ed., Seeing Things Whole, The Essential John Wesley Powell 350 (2001) from John Wesley Powell, "Competition as a Factor in Human Evolution" in The American Anthropologist 1/4 (October 1888): 297-323.

[4] Richard Tarnas, The Passion of the Western Mind, Understanding the Ideas That Have Shaped Our World View 270 (1991).

[5] The school awarded him an honorary master's degree, so that they could make Powell a faculty member to teach science. Donald Worster, A River Running West, The Life of John Wesley Powell 115 (2001).

[6] Tarnas at 421.

[7] William H. Goetzmann, New Lands, New Men, America and the Second Great Age of Discovery 405 (1986).

[8] Id. at 406.

[9] William H. Goetzmann, Exploration & Empire, The Explorer and the Scientist in the Winning of the American West 566 (1966).

[10] Quoted in Kinsey at 112, from Exploration of the Colorado River of the West. H. Misc. Doc. 300, 43rd Cong., 1st sess., 1873-74. Also published as Exploration of the Colorado River of the West and its Tributaries: Explored in 1869, 1870, 1871, and 1872, Under the Direction of the Secretary of the Smithsonian Institution, Washington: U.S. Government Printing Office, 1875, at 214.

[11] Kinsey at 114-115.

[12] Quoted in deBuys at 349 quoting from "Competition as a Factor in Human Evolution" in The American Anthropologist 1/4 (October 1888): 297-323.

[13] J.W. Powell, The Exploration of the Colorado River and its Canyons 394, 397 (Dover Publications Inc. 1961 Republication of Canyons of the Colorado 1895).

[14] Quoted in deBuys at 282, from Century Magazine 39 (April 1890): 915-22.

[15] In Commerce of the Prairies Josiah Gregg describes the acequia system by which the Hispanic settlers irrigated long narrow parcels abutting the stream from a mother ditch feeding smaller laterals to five or six acre fields. Operation and maintenance of the acequias was a community enterprise for the benefit of the community. Three hundred or more acequias were operating in New Mexico at the time Powell was exploring the West. Josiah Gregg, Commerce of the Prairies (1844) (Reprint of 1974, University of Oklahoma Press, Max L. Moorhead, ed., 107-108); New Mexico State Engineer's Office, Acequias, 4 (1997).

[16] deBuys at 100-102, "An Overland Trip to the Grand Canon," Scribner's Monthly 10/13 (October 1975): 659-78.

[17] deBuys at 109, "The Ancient Province of Tusayan," Scribner's Monthly 11 (1896): 193-213.

[18] Leonard J. Arrington and Dean May, "A Different Mode Of Life: Irrigation and Society in Nineteenth-Century Utah," in James H. Shideler, Editor, Agriculture in the Development of the Far West 7 (1975).

[19] Id. at 8.

[20] deBuys at 120.

[21] Goetzmann, Exploration & Empire at 569.

[22] Id. at 570.

[23] John Wesley Powell, Lands of the Arid Region of the United States (1983 Facsimile of the 1879 Edition).

[24] 1 Colo. 551 (1872)

[25] Colo. Const. Art. XVI, sections 5,6 & 7.

[26] Powell, Arid Lands at 42-43.

[27] Id. at 43.

[28] Worster, at 378.

[29] Id. at 371.

[30] Powell, Arid Lands at 10.

[31] William Gilpin, Colorado's first Territorial Governor, promoted Western settlement during a cycle of wet weather, proclaiming another of the Western great false prophecies: "rain follows the plow." Kinsey at 110. After President Lincoln removed him as Territorial Governor after one year in office, Gilpin became a land development, railroad, and irrigation proponent. In numerous speeches and writings that received nationwide attention, he argued, "Colorado's dryness was an advantage, for irrigated farming was the most efficient form of agriculture . . . ." Thomas L. Karnes, William Gilpin: Western Nationalist 318 (1970).

[32] Powell, Arid Lands at 11.

[33] Id. at 12–14.

[34] Powell, Arid Lands at 40–45; Worster at 479–86.

[35] David Lavender, Colorado River Country 173 (1982).

[36] De Buys at 214–15.

[37] Kinsey at 98; Worster at 356–58.

[38] Worster at 494–495.

[39] Wallace Stegner, Beyond the Hundreth Meridian, John Wesley Powell and the Second Opening of the West 227-28 (1954).

[40] Id. at 239.

[41] Id. at 303.

[42] John Wesley Powell, address, Official Report of the International Irrigation Congress 109 112 (1893), quoted in Worster, at 529 (2001).